ESTANCIAS

The Great Houses and Ranches of Argentina

ESTANCIAS

The Great Houses and Ranches of Argentina

Text by María Sáenz Quesada
Photographs by Xavier A. Verstraeten

Translated from the Spanish
by Norman Thomas di Giovanni

Compiled by Mercedes Villegas de Larivière,
Marina Larivière, Inés Baron Supervielle de Stegmann,
and Baroness Francesca von Thielmann

Abbeville Press   Publishers
New York   London   Paris

Jacket front: A groom tending one of the horses at La Bellaca's stud farm.
Jacket back: The living room at Tres Bonetes (see p. 21).
Front flap: The facade of San Nicolás (see p. 141).
Back flap: The gate at La Biznaga's old entrance (see p. 104).
Half-title page: The view from Huetel's front porch (see p. 79).
Frontispiece: The main house and garden at La Independencia (see p. 34).
Copyright page: A field of red peppers at La Angostura in Salta Province.

Editor: Jacqueline Decter
Designer: Molly Shields
Production Editor: Sarah Key
Production Manager: Dana Cole

Map by Sophie Kittredge
Photographs on pages 188–97 by Florian von der Fecht

Library of Congress Cataloging-in-Publication Data
Sáenz Quesada, María.
Estancias: the great houses and ranches of Argentina / text by
María Sáenz Quesada ; photographs by Xavier A. Verstraeten ;
compiled by Mercedes Villegas de Larivière . . . [et al.].
p.   cm.
Includes bibliographical references.
ISBN 1-55859-270-9
1. Haciendas—Argentina.   2. Farmhouses—Argentina.   3. Farm
buildings—Argentina.   I. Verstraeten, Xavier A.   II. Larivière,
Mercedes Villegas de.   III. Title.
NA8210.A7S24   1992
728.8'0982—dc20
92-16213
CIP

To the inhabitants, past and present, of rural Argentina: Indians, gauchos, landowners, herdsmen, and immigrant farmers; to the technicians who brought modern methods to agricultural production; to the writers and artists who reinvented nature; to the architects and landscape gardeners who designed the estancias' buildings and laid out their parks. Among them, they have created part of Argentine reality, part of Argentine myth.

BOLIVIA

Jujuy

Salta

Salta • 20
21
19

PARAGUAY

Formosa

Tucumán

Catamarca

Santiago del Estero

El Chaco

Paraná R.

Corrientes

Misiones

BRAZIL

La Rioja

Córdoba
16

Santa Fe

Entre Ríos

Uruguay R.

San Juan

Córdoba •

Santa Fe •
Paraná •
14
15

3

URUGUAY

Rosario •
17

11

3
8

San Luis

1

Buenos Aires •

Mendoza •

18

6
9

12
4
Salado R.
2

R. Plate

Mendoza

La Pampa

Buenos Aires

5

10
7

PACIFIC OCEAN

CHILE

ANDES OF THE

CORDILLERA

Neuquén

Limay R.

R. Negro

R. Negro

ATLANTIC OCEAN

L. Nahuel Huapi

22

Río Negro

Chubut

Santa Cruz

24

L. Argentino

Río Gallegos •

Str. of Magellan

Territory of Tierra del Fuego

23

R. Grande

Beagle Ch.

Falkland Islands
(Malvinas)

N

0   100   200   300   400   500 km

Contents

Acknowledgments

The publication of this book would not have been possible without the help and encouragement of a great many people—too many, unfortunately, to name individually here. Nevertheless, our deep and sincere thanks go first and foremost to the owners of the estancias, who offered us the hospitality and generosity for which Argentine landowners are justly renowned and who willingly shared with us their knowledge about the origins and history of their homes. We are also especially grateful to the staffs of the estancias for their unfailing kindness and enthusiasm.

Working closely with María Sáenz Quesada and Xavier A. Verstraeten has made us appreciate their dedication, which—in their words and photographs, respectively—has resulted in the achievement of everything we set out to do when this volume was first conceived.

We also extend thanks to Jean-Louis Larivière, our Buenos Aires publisher, and Jackie Decter, our New York editor, as well as to designer Molly Shields and translator Norman Thomas di Giovanni for their professionalism and unflagging commitment. We are indebted to Mark Magowan for believing in this project from the start and to Robert Abrams, our New York publisher, for backing it wholeheartedly.

Thank you also to Charles de Ganay, Jürgen Tesch, Hendrick te Neues, Michael Klett, and Bartholomew Sneeze.

We cannot conclude without expressing profound gratitude to Bonifacio del Carril, Yuyú Guzmán, Hernán Lavalle Cobo, Guillermo Martínez Udaondo, and Virginia Verstraeten for their continuous support and advice.

The Compilers

Introduction

To most Argentines, the word *estancia* brings to mind a number of images and deep-seated feelings about an agricultural system that is part and parcel of the country's history and that today, some three and a half centuries after the first settlement of its vast grassy plains, is still a vital force in the national economy.

In one of his most celebrated stories, woven from autobiographical snippets, Jorge Luis Borges touches upon the phenomenon of this shared Argentine past. Juan Dahlmann, the hero of "The South," has managed to hang on to his family estate somewhere in Buenos Aires Province. One of Dahlmann's habits of mind is to recall the medicinal smell of the estancia's eucalyptus trees and its long, dusky pink house, which had once been crimson. But work and perhaps indolence keep him on in the city. Summer after summer he takes pleasure in the abstract idea of ownership and in the certainty that his house is waiting for him at a fixed point on the plain. "Tomorrow I shall wake up at the estancia," he thinks one day, and in the end he makes the journey there, to some unspecified locale in the south, where he finds himself face to face with his destiny. In both his imagination and daydreams, Borges, like many of his fellow Argentines, gives the estancia a role—that of a bolt-hole, a place of refuge, with a good deal of the maternal lap about it, set down in the immensity of the plain. But Borges's is not the only view.

To the writer and naturalist W. H. Hudson, River Plate estancias were also a place of refuge, though they could prove quite dangerous. Such was the case of the establishment known as Vagabonds' Rest, in the half-savage Uruguayan hinterlands of Paysandú, where there was "not even a shade tree or cultivated plant of any description." Here, as the central figure of his novel *The Purple Land* finds out, skill with a knife could prove risky because a man would find his reputation as a fighter constantly tested by others who wanted to try their strength against his.

Between these two ways of viewing an estancia—Hudson's, which goes back a hundred or so years, and Borges's, from the 1950s—came a complicated period. During that interval the owners of rural property—the stockmen, or ranchers— turned the unending pampa into a system of highly productive farming units whose herdsmen and peons were subjected to more and more restriction and regulation, thereby spelling doom for the plain's refractory inhabitant, the gaucho. These events can be followed in the story of Martín Fierro, the eponymous hero of the poem by José Hernández published in the 1870s, and in *Don Segundo Sombra*, a novel written in the 1920s by Ricardo Güiraldes, himself the owner of an estancia.

Don Segundo, with his Indian complexion and spare frame, darkly and soberly dressed in the traditional way of country dwellers at the time, managed to reconcile his innate desire for freedom with the new pattern of existence demanded of ranch hands around the turn of the century. A drover and horsebreaker, Segundo sold his services to different establishments, and this made it possible for him to live not as a common laborer but as a free man on horseback.

The sentiments that the Argentine imagination associates with estancias are reinforced by nineteenth-century iconography. Images of Indian raiding parties, spears held high, making off with women and cattle, inspired the watercolors and drawings of Fernando Brambila, Emeric Essex Vidal, Carlos Morel, Juan Mauricio Rugendas, and Juan León Pallière, among others, and evoke the ferocity that once existed between whites and aboriginals along the wilderness frontier. Tinged with romanticism, these pictures have also handed down a particular impression of the work carried out on an estancia. In their paintings, Prilidiano Pueyrredón and Carlos Enrique Pellegrini popularized country scenes: the dance called the *cielito*, for example, in which couples are profiled against a boundless horizon; an open fire over which a piece of meat is roasting or a kettle boils for brewing maté. Much later, in the 1930s, the calendars illustrated by Florencio Molina Campos left a tender record, full of nostalgia and humor, of old-time Argentine country types, dressed in their baggy trousers, berets, and rope-soled canvas shoes. To Argentines, these characters are eternal, outside time, and when we look at them we see ourselves, our own setting.

Another part of the myth of the estancia stems from the early years of this century, when these rural establishments turned the Argentine Republic into one of the world's leading producers of meat and grain, and their owners became some of the richest men in the Western world. It was a splendid era. Argentine cattlemen frequented the Belle Epoque's most sophisticated capitals to buy Derby winners with which to found their own racing stables, while back at home they had themselves photographed alongside their own prize cattle. In those days, the parents of Victoria Ocampo, an upper-class writer and founder of the magazine *Sur*, crossed the Atlantic to Europe with numerous offspring, domestic staff, two cows, and a battery of hens so as to ensure a supply of fresh food during the voyage. Life was sweet for the wealthy ranch owner, who could lease his estates and spend long periods in Paris, untroubled by financial concerns. The uniqueness of Argentina's estancias began to gain fame abroad. "In fact, neither in England, where modern farming was created, nor in France, where we also have excellent, up-to-date establishments, is there anything like an Argentine estancia," wrote Jules Huret, *Le Figaro*'s globetrotting correspondent, who in 1910 visited a number of River Plate farms. But to understand what the word *estancia* means in Argentina today, where it is applied to rural properties of upwards of four hundred hectares (about a thousand acres), we must go back to the beginnings of European settlement in America.

The Spanish Crown, which claimed title to all conquered territory, granted land to the early settlers of what is now Argentina on the condition that, if it were near the capital, they grew crops on it or, if farther away (and so long as it did not interfere with the crops of Indians), they made it into an estancia and raised livestock on it. An estancia then consisted of about three square miles and was not strictly a piece of private property but meant the right to graze animals in a specified place. A brand mark was enough to secure the ownership of cattle, sheep, and horses, all of which—since there were no large mammals in the New World that could be domesticated—had been brought from Europe. Together with his herdsmen, a proprietor took free-ranging animals and confined, tamed, and accustomed them to a stamping ground. Only later would the owner apply to the government for title to the range on which his flocks or herds grazed. If he were a person of prestige or influence, possession was granted; if he were not, he became an intruder or squatter.

This same process, with regional variations, went on throughout Spanish America. In the seventeenth century, in the Andes, the word *hacienda* became the prevalent term for a privately owned rural property. Many such establishments were in the hands of religious orders, and on these farms the cultivation of crops—by paid,

Branding at Los Yngleses, early
twentieth century.

slave, or indentured labor—displaced stock breeding as the chief economic activity. What was produced went to local markets and only exceptionally, as in the case of hides, was anything sold outside the Spanish Empire. Meanwhile, in the River Plate provinces, the word *estancia* gradually came to refer not only to a particular use of the land but also to the land, or property, itself. Its owner could therefore call himself, interchangeably, an *estanciero* or an *hacendado*. He was a stockbreeder, for the most part of mules, which he raised for northern markets.

River Plate estancias enjoyed an exceptional setting, the grassy plain—or humid pampa—one of Argentina's seven biogeographic regions. The republic, which contains over a million square miles and extends some 2,200 miles from top to bottom, encompasses a range of different landscapes from the tropical north to the subantarctic south. Running west to east, the high peaks of the Andes descend to the plains—first arid, then humid—that stretch to the Paraná and the River Plate and end at the Atlantic shore. "Of our various landscapes one is dominant—the pampa, which makes us into plainsmen and people of a temperate climate," wrote the late Ricardo Rojas, one of Argentina's foremost men of letters. The first to point out the originality of gauchesco literature, Rojas was convinced that the land makes the race and that, through man, the race reveals the spirit of the place.

Pampa, the Quechua word for an open space or plain, refers in its widest sense as much to the bleak, stony plateaus of the Jujuy puna and the Córdoba sierra as to the temperate prairie. In general, however, the term applies more narrowly to the grassy rangelands of the provinces of Buenos Aires (except in the extreme south), Santa Fe (except in the extreme north), and parts of Córdoba, La Pampa, San Luis, and Entre Ríos, which is cut by a range of gentle hills called *cuchillas*.

In this vast area, which could easily contain the whole of France, rain falls throughout the year. To the casual observer the land seems uniform and monotonous, but someone with experience can distinguish the slightly rolling terrain near the Paraná River from the deep soil, excellent for crops, at the heart of the duny region of the southeast or from the low-lying basin of the Salado River, which is full of shallow lakes and wetlands. The humid pampa was originally covered by a coarse grass that provided livestock with little nourishment, but gradually this vegetation was replaced by tender grasses and clover. Nowadays the pampa supports extensive crops, and its ranges produce fine horses, cattle, and sheep. To the north, west, and south, where thorny scrub begins, agriculture is feasible only by irrigation.

Domingo Faustino Sarmiento, one of Argentina's foremost thinkers and statesmen, blamed all the nation's ills in the last century on the vast extent of its wilderness. "Immensity is the universal characteristic of the country," he wrote; "the plains, the woods, the rivers are all immense, and the horizon is always undefined, always lost in haze and delicate vapors which forbid the eye to mark the point in the distant perspective where the land ends and the sky begins."

In the days before man changed the face of the pampa, it was necessary to journey several leagues to find an ombu, the only tree (actually a gigantic shrub) that—to the traveler's delight—sprouted here and there on the plain. According to W. H. Hudson, whose birthplace near Buenos Aires was named after an avenue of twenty-five of these trees, the ombu's enormous girth, low horizontal branches, and sinuous buttressed trunk made a splendid playhouse for children. He also noted that, "having . . . many curious superstitions connected with it, it is a romance in itself."

In Hudson's time the shallow lakelets, overgrown with dense beds of sedges and bulrushes, were full of bird life, but in general the land was poor in mammal species. There were the carnivorous puma, which rarely attacks a man but is a great hunter of large domestic animals, guanacos, and deer; the *gato montés*, or wood cat, a smallish native feline; the vizcacha; the gray fox; the timid, social, mouse-colored cavy; the tuco-tuco, an extensive burrower; and the skunk, as showy as it is smelly.

"The avi-fauna is relatively much richer than the mammalia," wrote Hudson, a tireless observer of the habits of birds. The pampa was home to the *ñandú*, or rhea, "the grand archaic ostrich of America [that] survives from a time when there were also giants among the avians," and to the nearly flightless tinamou, a partridgelike bird whose color blends with the drab tones of the plain. The marshes, streamlets, and lakes were a paradise for storks, ibises, herons, spoonbills, flamingos, and at least twenty species of the duck order, including beautiful black-necked and coscoroba swans. There were also the courlan, called "crazy widow" because of its mourning plumage, and the noisy lapwing. The crested caracara, almost the size of an eagle, and its humble companion, the drab *chimango*, were both common species of the pampa, which from September on receives migrating birds from as far away as North America and the Arctic. Another aquatic species was the *chajá*, or crested screamer, which pours forth its notes by day and also sings by night—"counting the hours," according to gaucho lore.

Native flora and fauna supplied the modest needs of the bands of Indians, who roamed the plain dressed in hides and armed with bolas. A people with no tradition of farming, they pitched tents on the shores of streams or lakes. But the Spaniard's eating habits required wheat and beef, and he needed the horse to shorten distances. The arrival of domestic livestock, a gift of the conquistadors, brought about a peaceful revolution on the pampa and gave the countryside a new, unsuspected dimension. In the flat wilderness, covered in coarse grass and riddled with vizcacha burrows, where a man on foot is lost, the horse—according to the Scottish writer Robert Cunninghame Graham, who marveled at the skill of the Argentine rider—was a godsend. As for the cow, from colonial times on it became the most important staple of national life. "We should worship it, like the Hindus and ancient Egyptians," remarked the writer Ezequiel Martínez Estrada, a follower of Sarmiento, "because from the cow come nearly all our wealth and all our ills."

In early colonial times, it was incumbent upon the founder of each city to set out the boundaries of the first farms and estancias. Soon it became evident that the best site for an estancia was a protected spot along the banks of one of the lazy, meandering watercourses of the pampa, preferably a nook or bend, known locally as a *rincon*, where the cattle, being more easily confined, readily established their stamping ground. Early Buenos Aires landowners occupied a segment of land somewhere in the arc that stretched south of the city for twenty leagues and from east to west for sixty or seventy. Each plot was rectangular in shape, half a league (2.5 kilometers, or 1.56 miles) wide by a league and a half (7.5 kilometers, or 4.69 miles) deep. This amounted to some 1,875 hectares (7.24 square miles) for each estancia, an area suitable for grazing a thousand head. There, with treading and trampling by the stock, the grass began to improve.

The early estancia was centered around the *rascadero*, a hardwood post, driven into the ground, that attracted the cattle and against which they could scratch themselves. The proprietor also placed salt here to compensate for the lack of it in the pampa soil. "The vast, brown, open space, sometimes a quarter of a mile across, called *el rodeo* . . . was the centre of the life of the great cattle estancias of the plains," wrote Cunninghame Graham. "To it on almost every morning of the year the cattle were collected and taught to stand there till the dew was off the grass."

In outlying districts, however, stock was vulnerable to marauding Indians. In the vast setting of the pampa, where the leading actors were the forces of nature—sun, light, air, wind—the presence of new riches in horses and cattle brought discord between the whites and the Indians. Both wanted these descendants of the original livestock, introduced by the Spaniards, that now roamed the plains in a semi-wild state. This coveted booty kindled a war that was fought intermittently on the pampa until the 1870s, when the Argentine government, in a concerted military campaign, brought about the final "Conquest of the Desert," the name given to the systematic extermination of the Indians.

Up until then, security had been the landowner's most serious problem. This made him build his makeshift dwelling on open, elevated ground, from which he could detect the faintest sign—a slight cloud of dust, perhaps—of the presence of the Indian foe, who had become as good or better a rider than the Spaniard. A number of outposts, located on an estancia's perimeters—each inhabited by a herdsman and his family—served both as lookouts and as stations from which to manage the herds.

Occasionally landowners got together in joint ventures. In the seventeenth and eighteenth centuries, the most typical of these was the *vaquería*, a hunting party licensed by the local cabildo, in which wild cattle were pursued, either to be slaughtered for their hides or to be rounded up for branding and taming. Salt-gathering convoys were another shared undertaking. At an appointed time of the year, a large party set off for the great salt lakes nearly four hundred miles southwest of Buenos Aires. One such caravan in 1810 consisted of 230 wagons, 3,000 oxen, 400 men, and 500 horses. Care was taken in crossing Indian land, and the leaders of these wagon trains became justly renowned, for on the pampa, where morning and evening the sun rises and sets on a horizon not unlike that of the sea, finding one's way required skill and experience. An evocation of the Argentine plains by Cunninghame Graham corroborates this:

> A grassy sea, in which the landmarks were the stars, so that a man rode straighter in the night than in full noontide, if he had lost his way. A green illimitable sea, in which the horse was ship; a desert without camels, but as terrible to wander in as is the Sahara, in which the horseman who had lost his trail was swallowed up and never heard of, except some traveller chance to find his skull, just sticking out of a dark tuft of grass.

The easiest way to set up an estancia was simply to take possession of the land. Eventually, by paying money to the state, the squatter could obtain a title, especially if he showed a willingness to lend his services in fighting the Indians. Not all such aspirants succeeded, however. Many owners of small properties, with but a few hundred head of cattle, had not the means to bring complicated claims before a registry official. Unless the law took pity on them, they could be driven off the land by men with power and political influence in the city. It was the large landholding, in short, that was sanctioned as the most acceptable and therefore most desirable form of ownership. Thus, certain colonial officials labored in vain to prevent the wholesale dividing up of the public domain among a few proprietors. What these officials had recommended instead was that it be distributed free as homesteads to the landless so as to incorporate them into civilized society and to raise the general level of prosperity while at the same time securing Argentina's frontiers against the Indians and the Portuguese.

Up until this time, the country's most successful estates had been those of the Society of Jesus, whose products provided sustenance for the Jesuits' own monasteries, schools, and Indian settlements. The fathers themselves marketed the goods—including woolen cloth woven in their own workshops—and taught the Indians animal husbandry. When the Crown expropriated the Jesuits and expelled them from the country in 1767, some of their properties passed into private hands.

Then, in the last decades of the eighteenth century, the economy of the River Plate began to expand at a significant pace. Two factors contributed to this: the strategic importance that Buenos Aires had acquired within the Viceroyalty of the

A volanta, *once widely used in the Argentine countryside, crosses a swampy creek at Los Yngleses around 1920.*

Río de la Plata as a result of increasing penetration by the Portuguese and British into the area; and the appeal that cattle breeding took on with the Free Trade Regulation of 1778, which opened the ports of Buenos Aires and Montevideo to trade with Spain and the Americas. Up until then, cowhides and horsehides, the principal wealth of the estancia since the days of the *vaquería*, had enjoyed only limited access to foreign markets, since the bulk of trade between the pampa and Spain had by order to be conducted via Peru and the Pacific Ocean across Panama and the Caribbean.

The lifted restrictions on what could now be shipped abroad by direct sea routes brought an era of prosperity to the pampa estancias, which quickly sought outlets beyond domestic markets. On the northern haciendas of the viceroyalty, however, the cattle continued to be bred only for local consumption in accordance with the region's old subsistence economy. Toward the end of the colonial period new enterprises appeared on the pampa. One of the most profitable, which sprang up along the shores of the Paraná River, was the breeding of mules for use as pack and saddle animals, particularly in mountainous areas like Bolivia, where they were much in demand in the silver mines. Another industry of the time was beef-salting, which produced jerked beef and salted meat as well as hides and tallow.

By now, the Río de la Plata, one of Imperial Spain's most far-flung colonies, had begun to acquire local decision-making powers. This in turn led to demands for greater financial autonomy from the heartland of the province, where a new generation of landowners, many recently arrived in the country, had begun to apply urban business principles to stockraising. The Anchorena, Obligado, Ramos Mexía, Martínez de Hoz, Alzaga, and García de Zúñiga families, among others, were all of this generation. After the colony gained its independence (1810–16), the new professional class of landowner, whose initial wealth had derived from trade, began its long, dramatic rise to a far-reaching influence, one still felt in Argentina today.

Meanwhile, it fell to the less exalted estancia owner, who saw his role as bringing order to that unending, empty space that was the pampa, to officiate as a kind of link between the urban and rural worlds, between the polarities that Sarmiento characterized as civilization and barbarism. This type of landowner was responsible for the Christian upbringing of all those on his estate and the surrounding area. If the estancia were large it might have a chapel or an oratory where on occasion mass was said and local people gathered to be married or baptized. In his life of the caudillo Facundo, arguably the most famous work of Argentine literature, Sarmiento has painted this portrait of one such cattleman:

> In 1838 I happened to be in the sierra of San Luis, at the home of a landowner whose two favorite occupations were saying prayers and gambling. He had built a chapel where on Sunday afternoons, to supply the want of a priest and the divine service which the place had not seen for many years, he prayed through the rosary. It was a Homeric picture: the sun declining to the west; the sheep returning to the fold and rending the air with their confused bleatings; the service conducted by the master of the house, a man of sixty, with a noble countenance, in which the pure European race was evident in the white skin, blue eyes, and serene broad forehead; while the responses were made by a dozen women and some young men, whose imperfectly broken horses were tied near the chapel door.

Such a patriarch was an ideal candidate for the post of Alcalde de Hermandad, in colonial times a sort of rural police chief and after independence a justice of the peace. He had little choice but to enroll in the militia if he wanted to protect his family and stock in the event of either an Indian attack or an invasion by foreign troops. He was not a feudal lord in the medieval European sense, but his position had certain seigneurial elements and his social standing was far higher than that of the small landowner or the gaucho. He did not attempt to found a dynasty—that is, to link his name to the land. But as his property would be divided equally among his heirs, he did his best to acquire enough land to prevent his sons from having to become pen pushers in the city. So long as he was able to, he owned slaves, because he needed them to look after his vegetable garden and tend his animals. His relations with the gaucho, whose skills he admired and respected, were complicated; for the landowner was committed to turning the gaucho into a law-abiding farmhand. To this end, he obliged the gauchos, who roamed the countryside, to carry a *papeleta de conchabo*, a document stating where and for whom they worked.

As a social group, the large landowners solved many of the practical problems of life on the pampa and steadily became richer and more powerful. But even while their old way of life changed, they jealously preserved evidence of their past, such as the crumbling ruins of early buildings that still lurk in the woodlands of the most up-to-date estancias. Their first concern had been to secure title to the land; next they had to find ways to circumvent the heavy taxes that the government levied and that the cattlemen always considered excessive, even in periods when their profits were rising. Rural isolation was another serious problem, affecting both proprietor and farmhand. Conscientious landowners were always fearful of the *pulpería*, or country-store-cum-saloon, where local people gathered to drink and play cards in an attempt to escape the melancholy of their lonely existence. Drink was often the ruination of peons and of their masters' weaker, more wayward sons. Finally, dominating the whole scene, was the war against Indian depradations, for on its favorable outcome depended access to new fertile land, safe travel, and—above all—life itself. This was a constant struggle in which robbery, enslavement, or massacre awaited the loser.

For his estancia to be successful, a landowner had to be both a countryman and a man of the city. In outward appearance, however, there might be little difference between the master and the gaucho. Both dressed in the *chiripá*, a kind of loincloth worn instead of trousers over fringed pantaloons, poncho, neckerchief, and a wide belt studded with rows of silver ornamentation. Both aspired to the finest saddle gear, but in materials and quality there could be a substantial difference. The fine vicuña wool of the owner's poncho, for example, was superior to the homespun that a cowhand wore. In the early days, a thatched adobe hut was the dwelling common to both rich and poor. Built of perishable materials found on the pampa—mud, straw, reeds, hides for covering doors and windows, and on rare occasions timber—such buildings were as easy to erect as to abandon. From the point of view of the gaucho, who was loath to settling in one place, this shelter was adequate for women and children. He slept outdoors, his ear cocked for dangers that lurked in the night. The owner, however, had to set an example. His hut would be more elaborate and he would have several: one for himself and his family, who spent the spring and summer months on the estate; another for his farm manager; and others for tools and equipment.

The center of an old Argentine estancia was the hearth. Here the embers always glowed, a kettle was kept on the boil for brewing maté, and there was a place for planting a spit into the earth floor for barbecuing beef, the basic food of the plains. A short distance away was the corral, ringed by a dry moat or palisade. This was the classic setting for much of the work of the estancia, such as horsebreaking and cattle branding, activities that brought together neighboring ranch hands as well as an establishment's own slaves and herdsmen. Such gatherings had their origins in the bygone days of the cattle hunts, when to the native-born Argentine all work was a kind of sport in which everyone galloped at full speed and the skill lay in hamstringing a cow with a single blow. The legendary gaucho Martín Fierro was to look back with nostalgia on that bygone period, when rural chores seemed more fun than work. Early English ranchers noted with dismay that lasso-brandishing gauchos often joined in the roundup for the sheer joy of it and would not accept any pay. In fact, much of Argentine folk music and dance can be linked to these gatherings in which animals were branded and castrated. The same is true of gauchesco poetry and the singing contests among gaucho bards, who improvised verses about deeds and events both real and imaginary. The subjects of the pampa and the gaucho are at the heart of Argentine literature and are dealt with extensively in the poetry of such figures as Bartolomé Hidalgo, Hilario Ascasubi, and José Hernández in the last century, and in the novels of Benito Lynch and Ricardo Güiraldes in this.

Following the Revolution of 1810 and the collapse of Spanish rule, Argentina's great landed families acquired hitherto undreamed-of political power. A number of these ranch owners, local strongmen with their own bands of gaucho militia, led some of the rival factions of the day. It was a stormy, complicated period that involved a succession of opponents with a range of political views: *directoriales* and *artiguistas*, Unitarians and Federals, *apostólicos* and *lomos negros*. In the bloody civil war that followed the seven-year struggle for independence and continued right up to the battle of Pavón in 1861, the majority of ranchers sided with the Federal Party, which wanted to structure the country into a loose federation of semi-autonomous provinces somewhat along the lines of the United States.

The chief of the *federales*, of course, was the ranch owner Juan Manuel de Rosas, a leader of extraordinary faculties who ruled Argentina from 1829 to 1832 and 1835 to 1852, although nominally he was only governor of Buenos Aires. His brand of federalism, however, had deeply traditional Hispanic roots. Another leading *federal*—but with overtones of economic and cultural liberalism—was Justo José de Urquiza, the Entre Ríos landowner who in 1852 defeated Rosas in the battle of Caseros and from 1854 to 1860 served as Argentina's first constitutional president.

Political loyalties shifted, both before and after this period, but as a class the landowners never lost their power. Their vast holdings originated in good part as a result of the law of emphyteusis, passed by the province of Buenos Aires in 1821, during the administration of Bernardino Rivadavia, an early Unitarian. The law, by which vast tracts of public land were rented to individuals, was intended to promote agriculture—including small and middle-sized farms—but in fact it chiefly benefited the great cattle breeders, urban entrepreneurs attracted by an enterprise that demanded little initial capital and yielded large profits. Fifteen years later, Governor Rosas—Rivadavia's bitterest foe—sold off the leased public land to those occupying it, thereby enabling them to consolidate their fortunes.

When the writer and educator Domingo Faustino Sarmiento became Argentina's president in 1868, his plans included a law to help immigrants settle on small holdings that would be given over to growing crops. However, owing to the opposition of the great landowners, who were now national and provincial senators and congressmen, the bill was defeated. A further instance of the ranchers' near monopoly of the land can be cited. When army officers were awarded tracts in recognition of their services in the Indian wars, they sold them to city entrepreneurs, thus giving rise to

another generation of *estancieros*. Of course, some agricultural schemes for settling foreigners on the land were successful, primarily in the provinces of Entre Ríos and Santa Fe, with a few others in Córdoba and Buenos Aires.

By the turn of the century estancias could be found over the length and breadth of Argentina, all the way from the Lerma valley of Salta, in the extreme northwest, where maize, alfalfa, and fruit were grown and heifers were fattened, to the remote ends of the earth, in Tierra del Fuego. There, on the Beagle Channel, the missionary Thomas Bridges had founded an establishment on land granted to him by the government. In Patagonia, where the Tehuelche and Araucanian tribes had been virtually exterminated, new estancias were founded exclusively for sheep raising. Most of the hands who worked on these ranches were, and still are, Chileans.

The modernization of the pampa came about as a result of technological advances that were incorporated into farming by those landowners who saw the need to adapt production methods to the requirements of world trade. The widespread use of the windmill, a cheap source of energy for watering cattle, permitted the opening up of the virgin prairies of the west, which had been taken from the Indians in 1879. The invention of refrigeration by Charles Tellier made possible the export of frozen meat and launched the meat-packing industry, thus increasing the value of the estancias' main product. Improved transportation also accelerated the process of modernization. By 1910 the railroads covered a large part of the country, and crossing the Atlantic became quicker and cheaper thanks to improvements in steamship travel. A system of mixed crops, combined with crop rotation every three years—a practice that began around 1890—made it possible to alternate grain fields with pastureland. Immigrant farmers, who built themselves humble dwellings on land rented from the large estancias, first sowed wheat, then maize, and finally alfalfa, so that when their leases ran out the owner—at little expense to himself—got his land back in an improved state.

Wagons loaded with wool at Los Yngleses around the turn of the century.

Now that the pampa was settled and towns that had once been frontier forts prospered, thousands of immigrant families, with their various languages, customs, and beliefs, began to absorb native Argentine traditions. To these impoverished European peasants, the pampa looked more and more like the promised land. Although these changes upset those who yearned for the time when the plains were virgin soil, from the economic point of view their settlement became highly profitable. At the outset of this century, when sheep farming declined and flocks were relegated to Patagonia, cattle raising was carried out on an industrial scale, and model estancias were awarded prizes at the annual shows of the Sociedad Rural, a prestigious breeders' association founded in 1866. By the teens of this century, Argentina figured in the first rank of the world's exporters of meat and grain.

Jules Huret's remarks, quoted earlier, belong to this period of splendor, but staunch admirers of raw nature had another attitude toward progress. Cunninghame Graham, who had always found something unearthly about the Argentine plains and now felt the loss of untrammeled freedom, lamented that "the whole pampa from the Romero Grande to Nahuel-Huapi and far Patagones is cut into innumerable chess-boards of wire fencing, and railways puff across it, taking up wool and corn and hides and other merchandise, to send to Europe." In fact, the reality and myth of the Argentine estancia is contained in both these views.

After the economic depression of the 1930s, the Argentine economy, based as it was on agriculture, would never regain its former prosperity. Around 1940, in a world that was hungry and at war, farming did enjoy a resurgence, but in the postwar period technological advances, protective tariffs abroad, and even changes in taste altered the demand for Argentine exports. Nor was policy at home conducive to an increase in agricultural exports. To begin with, in 1944 Juan Perón—then Secretary of Labor—introduced legislation to raise farm workers' wages and benefits. Then, from 1946 to 1955, during Perón's presidency, the government embarked on a program of industrial expansion that was underpinned by taxes levied on agricultural exports. (With one or two exceptions, import and export controls persisted into subsequent administrations.) At the same time, a freeze on farm rents and the extension of farm leases disrupted the estancieros' comfortable old system of absentee ownership and easy income. The immediate response of the landowners was to reduce investment in agriculture. Some, however, began to run their establishments themselves, and they succeeded in reorganizing them so as to bring in the increased yields that present-day farming requires.

This book presents photographs and short accounts of a number of Argentina's largest and most characteristic estancias. Each was founded before 1914, and all have ties with Argentina's principal landed families. Retaining some of their early closeness to nature, most of these establishments remain the highly developed cattle-breeding units they have been since the estancia's heyday around the turn of the century. Nearly a hundred years later, much of the history of the Argentine countryside—with all its ups and downs, with all the changes that have taken place in Argentine society and the world—continues to be found in the stories of the great estancias. While theirs is no longer the only form of farming practiced in Argentina, it is the one that has had the greatest impact on the country's political, economic, and social history. And it is still the one most closely associated in the Argentine mind with the concept of a place of refuge and serenity.

Tres Bonetes

The humid pampa, the heartland of Argentina's estancias and one of the world's most fertile plains, stretches in a three-hundred-mile radius from the Argentine capital to include nearly the whole of Buenos Aires Province and parts of the adjoining provinces of La Pampa, Córdoba, Santa Fe, and Entre Ríos. Here, in a "practically infinite expanse of grassy desert, another sea," as the writer W. H. Hudson described this virgin territory, it was once estimated that it took no more than a foreman and ten cowherds on some sixty to seventy-five square miles to look after ten thousand head of cattle. With ample natural resources at hand and a relatively small amount of capital needed for livestock production, it was only a matter of time before the demands of world markets would bring the pampa region and its rural establishments (as Argentine estancias are also known) the fabled wealth they came to know in the golden years from 1880 to 1930.

The story of Tres Bonetes begins in the 1860s. At the time, ranchers were culling

Left: The main house, originally built in the late 1860s, was first remodeled in the Hispanic style at the end of the last century, but its crowning neocolonial touches were added only after 1930. The lookout tower, or mirador, now stands as a reminder of an earlier period, when there was danger from marauding Indians.

Right: The multicolored majolica-tiled dado of the living room walls is a common feature of Spanish interiors but unusual in an Argentine estancia. The mantelpiece is original to the house.

stock from their estates close to Buenos Aires or driving it to less expensive land farther inland. There they would first raise cattle, which was a means of trampling and improving the virgin grassland, after which they brought in flocks of sheep. The real wealth of the day lay in wool. Three friends and partners of Irish and Scottish descent, accompanied by a captive Indian who was acting as their guide, had made their way west in search of new land. Driving a troop of piebalds before them (in those days, for long-distance travel, a party of three would have had three or four mounts apiece, together with a mare to keep the spare horses close by), they plunged into the pampa wilderness beyond Junín, then an army garrison known as Fort Federación. The place they were looking for, three *bonetes*—"bonnets" in Spanish; in the Argentine, also a kind of headgear worn by gaucho militiamen, hence by extension a hillock, or knoll—was close to a pair of shallow lakes.

Fixing the estancia's boundaries, they returned to Buenos Aires to apply to the government for title to the land, which was granted in 1868. By then the district of Lincoln, named after the recently assassinated president of the United States, had been created. The estate consisted of 12 square leagues (30,000 hectares, or about 115 square miles). The title was issued in the name of Héctor Mackern, a native of County Limerick, Ireland.

Once the sale was legalized, every necessity was brought in: livestock, work horses, building materials, provisions, pots and kettles, spits, branding irons. The cattle were divided into two herds and, in keeping with the old custom, for each a post of *ñandubay*—a native hardwood—was sunk into the ground.

Neighboring Indians, however, were displeased, and from the outset relations

Left: Entrance to the coach house, built in the 1930s as a shed. The posts are of quebracho, a hardwood from the northern provinces. The traditional reds and dusky pinks of Argentine rural buildings are said to have been derived from a mixture of lime wash and cows' blood.

Right: This later addition to the rear part of the house looks out onto a quiet nook of the garden and is used for storing riding gear. The grilled windows are another Spanish touch. A hundred years earlier they would have served as a defense against thieves and Indian raids.

between them and the estancia owners were tinged with mutual distrust. On occasion the establishment sustained raids, putting the ranchers' fortitude and mettle to the test. Eventually, with the decimation of the Indians in the campaign known to Argentine history as the Conquest of the Desert, Tres Bonetes entered a period of prosperity.

In 1899 the estancia was acquired by Eduardo P. Maguire, a grandson of Irish immigrants, whose family, like so many other Irish, settled in Exaltación del Señor, a sheep-raising area near Buenos Aires. With eight brothers and sisters, he stood little chance of receiving a sizable inheritance so he set out selling sheep and eventually came to possess a fortune in land—some 386 square miles spread over several districts in the western reaches of Buenos Aires Province. Tres Bonetes, now consisting of over 30 square miles, with its horses and herds of shorthorns and Aberdeen Angus, became one of the province's leading estancias.

In 1930 Eduardo's eight children were bequeathed vast tracts of land. John Walter Maguire, who inherited Tres Bonetes, had absorbed a good deal of old lore as a boy when he listened around the hearth to gaucho and Indian cowhands telling stories

Left: Originally a sheep ranch, Tres Bonetes now raises shorthorns and Aberdeen Angus.

Right: Modern-day gauchos at rest under a cover of paraíso trees. The elaborate rastra, a kind of decorated belt buckle often worked in silver or gold or studded with coins, was once typical dress of Argentine farmhands. The knife, formerly a type of dagger called a facón, is worn over the kidney with the handle close to the right elbow.

of frontier days. He learned all about the famous Indian horseman Nahuel Payún, a cacique guide who was rich in cattle and a skilled silversmith—a craft the Pampa Indians knew well. The boy also learned of the beautiful "white lady," kidnapped by Indians, who haunted the house and park at night. Swooning and dying as her captors galloped off with her, she was buried on one of the estancia's knolls.

Fired by such tales, at the age of seventeen John Walter began to collect old silver riding gear. His first acquisition was a pair of stirrups. It was a time when the work of native-born artisans was undervalued. When pinched for money, the gauchos would put their gear up for sale in country saloons (which doubled in those days as general stores) or pawn it in the city. Maguire assembled an impressive collection of local silver—some of it worked by Indians—gold coins, and paintings by River Plate artists. Two books written by him, *Loncagüé* and *La pezuña de oro (The Golden Hoof)* attest to his abiding interest in the customs, legends, and crafts of the pampa.

Tres Bonetes was decorated by John Walter's wife, Susana Duhau, mother of the estancia's present owner, Susana Maguire Duhau. The windows in the ground-floor rooms were enlarged to provide more light and to better show off the colonial Portuguese furniture and the family collection of drawings, watercolors, and oils. Certain rooms have the air of a museum. One hallway is hung with ribbons and documents of the Federal period as well as with the shackles worn by Camila O'Gorman, whose illicit affair with a priest was punished by death in 1848. A trophy room, its floor paved with the anklebones of cows, displays spurs used by the Rioja caudillo Vicente "Chacho" Peñaloza. This was formerly the *matera*, the farmhands' kitchen, where gaucho cowherds sipped maté by the big open hearth. The estancia also boasts a collection of old carriages, harnesses, ox carts, and even a stagecoach.

Tres Bonetes 27

Rincón de López

"The place is a delight, full of little springs that form a brook, which flows into the Salado, which in turn flows into the River Plate. . . . The soil is good, and, unlike elsewhere, there are no ants here to destroy the crops. The locality is also rich in boar, partridge, wild dogs that look like tapirs, ostriches (smaller than their African counterparts), and horses without number."

This was the tenor of letters written in 1740, in which Jesuit fathers described what was one day to become the estancia known as Rincón de López, in the present district of Castelli, over a hundred miles to the southeast of Buenos Aires. There the Jesuits founded a settlement of converted Indians, Nuestra Señora de la Limpia Concepción del Salado, but some twenty years later withdrew because of the depradations of unsubjugated Indians. Today the estate belongs to descendants of one of the owners who succeeded the missionaries.

In the years before wire fencing, when there were few natural obstacles to prevent

Left: Facade of Rincón de López, one of Argentina's most historically rich estancias. In the early days, the mirador would have looked out on a treeless plain.

Right: The tower wall, clad in Virginia creeper, and the stone steps, brick paving, and wickerwork furniture all contribute to the classic serenity associated with old estancias.

stock from roaming widely, the most coveted estancias were those known as *rincones* (secluded corners or nooks), stretches of land located in the bend of a river or between two rivers, thereby forming a natural corral and easing the burden of keeping track of stock as well as reducing the number of hands such work required. Since the land in this particular coastal area was low and subject to periodic flooding, it was perfect for livestock but not for agriculture.

Around 1760, the site of what was then known as Rincón del Salado was taken over from the Jesuits by a soldier-cattleman, don Clemente López de Osornio. He was ready to defend the still unappropriated land against "vermin and wild Indians," with the aim of one day gaining legal title to it. The establishment took on a quasi-military aspect. Each of its *puestos*, where a watchman lived with his family, was furnished with firearms, and drawbridges were thrown over streams that served as defensive moats. Don Clemente grew rich making periodic excursions south of the Salado to round up or take hides from the cattle that roamed wild and he also supplied Buenos Aires with meat. In 1783, wanting to settle accounts with him, marauding Pampa Indians razed the estancia, spearing both owner and son and cutting their throats. But these dramatic events did not thwart the advance of settlement. López's daughter, Agustina, and her husband, León Ortiz de Rozas, continued her father's work. She spent long periods at the estancia dealing personally with the foremen and even tallying the livestock herself, a job that no good landowner left to anyone else.

The area was eventually pacified, and in 1811 León received title to part of the vast property that his father-in-law had occupied. At the time, the couple's son Juan Manuel (who was later slightly to alter the spelling of his surname to Rosas) ran the

Left: Portrait of a farmhand. Among the wide variety of headgear worn by Argentine countrymen through the years, the beret is a relatively recent arrival, dating from the 1840s. It arrived with Basque cowherds.

Right: In the somewhat austere dining room, the colonial silver on the sideboard and the simple wooden shutters add touches of restrained elegance.

ranch. In that territory south of the Indian frontier, Rosas gained authority over others by feats of strength and skill as a horseman as well as by his capacity to play a leading part in rural life. In the words of one English historian, "Rosas was a great politician, a rich *estanciero*, an owner of slaughtering establishments, and a soldier . . . who could deal equally well on his own terms with a cowboy and a foreign ambassador."

For six or so years the property was owned by one Braulio Costa, until it was bought in 1830 by Gervasio Rozas, Agustina and León's younger son, a critic of the dictatorial style of his brother Juan Manuel, who served as governor and captain-general, and ultimately absolute dictator of the province in the years 1829–33 and 1835–52. Gervasio turned Rincón into a model establishment, preparing jerked beef and shipping it directly abroad. The famous painter Prilidiano Pueyrredón paid long visits, leaving watercolors of the house, and rebellious young men of Buenos Aires society were sent to the estancia to be disciplined under Gervasio's watchful eye. Such were the cases of Bartolomé Mitre, the country's future president, and Lucio V. Mansilla, the author of one of Argentina's greatest books, *Una excursión a los indios ranqueles*.

Childless himself, Gervasio bequeathed the estancia to his friends Casto Sáenz Valiente and Juana Ituarte Pueyrredón de Sáenz Valiente, the great-grandparents of Rincón de López's present owners. Today, on its nine or so square miles, the estate produces Aberdeen Angus, the favorite breed of ranchers in this part of the province.

To lessen the problem of flooding, in 1910 the Waterways Commission moved the course of the Salado away from the house. The construction of a bridge over the river in the 1930s alleviated the need for *señuelos*, oxen trained to swim the river ahead of herds, which followed them without panic. On one part of the estancia, a veritable sanctuary for native fauna, it is still possible to catch a glimpse of a *gato montés*, a native species of wildcat.

Painted the typical rose pink—a color originally derived from mixing bulls' blood and whitewash—the house and outbuildings are impressive in the way they contrast with the park's crushed-shell paths and the deep green of vine-covered walls and century-old elms. A drawbridge over the stream stands as a silent witness to the estancia's heroic past, when Indian and rancher fought it out for use of the land and its cattle.

La Independencia
El Castillo

The main houses of La Independencia and El Castillo are set a short distance apart on the high wooded bluffs of the Paraná River, where the two estancias enjoy the magnificent spectacle of the sun rising out of the water and setting on the plain. The locale, a famous bend in the river known as La Vuelta de Obligado, was the scene of the battle in November 1845 between Argentine forces and Anglo-French gunboats trying to open up commercial navigation on the river, which Juan Manuel de Rosas considered the exclusive right of Argentina. In a nine-hour action, shore batteries fired on the foreign ships, but ultimately the Argentine guns were silenced and the day lost. The London *Times* was quick to record this early instance of the effective use of steam power in river warfare. A small monument at the foot of the bluff commemorates the episode.

Located near San Pedro, in the nothernmost tip of the province of Buenos Aires, these properties are among the few in the humid pampa that have been continuously

Left: La Independencia's mirador, which once signaled to vessels on the Paraná River below, rises above a luxuriant garden and vine-draped porch.

Right: The magnificent park on the bluffs above the Paraná overlooks the site of a battle in 1845 during the Anglo-French blockade of Buenos Aires. The Argentines lay three chains, supported by twenty-four ships, across the 800-yard-wide river, but still the enemy forces broke through.

Above: A corner of the dining room features an ancestral portrait and an early architectural rendering of the house.

Left: La Independencia's principal rooms open onto a long porch, fitted in bygone days with an elaborate iron grill for protection from thieves who plied the river.

Right: Doorway from the porch into the living room. The painting by Elena Obligado de Davel, mother of La Independencia's present owner, is of the Pueyrredón villa in San Isidro, on the outskirts of Buenos Aires.

PAGES 38–39
Left: A tangle of willows and ceibos along the edge of the Paraná. The vegetation in the water is one of four different species called the camalote, a common floating plant of Argentine lakes and rivers, especially of quiet backwaters.

Right: El Castillo has been home to the Obligados, a family of poets, for generations. When Rafael Obligado's wife became entranced with the Gothic novels of Sir Walter Scott, he built her this Scottish-style castle, complete with ivied turrets and battlements.

handed down through the male line. The original grant, known as Rincón de Andújar, was acquired in 1779 by don Antonio de Obligado, an Andalusian merchant who lived in Buenos Aires. He paid 15,000 gold pesos for nearly 175 square miles, together with 700 head of cattle. Don Antonio chose the estancia as a place to breed mules and cattle. The land was fertile, free of the scourge of Indians, and enjoyed easy river access to the capital of the new Viceroyalty of the Río de la Plata, the region's only center of commerce.

Juan José, one of don Antonio's children, eventually inherited the establishment and built the main house. He called it La Independencia, a name with a patriotic ring. Its thick walls and corniced mirador, or tower, are surrounded by *paraíso* trees, and a grape arbor overhangs the gallery. In the last century—until trade between the small towns along the Paraná declined—a flag would be hoisted over the mirador to indicate that there were goods to be shipped, especially wool.

Rafael Obligado, the author of *Santos Vega*, one of the most famous poems of gaucho life, belonged to the third generation of owners. "The Singer of the Paraná," as he became known in the annals of Argentine literature, loved the landscape of lazy creeks and the blossom of the blood-red *ceibo*—the Argentine national flower— and he evoked the place in these simple lines:

> *O beloved islands, sweet refuge*
> *of my boyhood years!*
> *Ancient algarrobos, old talas*
> *where the golden-winged cacique taught me to sing!*

His library is still at the estancia. Although at heart a staunch nativist, when it came to building a new house, don Rafael flattered his wife, Isabel Gómez Langeheim—

a passionate reader of the Gothic novels of Walter Scott—and erected El Castillo, the baronial castle, complete with turrets and battlements, whose exotic silhouette rises high above the Paraná bluffs. The work was carried out between 1896 and 1898 under the supervision of architect Eduardo Buttner.

El Castillo is typical of the romantic taste prevalent at the turn of the century, when wealth from the land reached its peak. Argentine estancias everywhere sprouted flamboyant examples of their owners' private fantasies. Often these emulated buildings glimpsed during tours of Europe, although it is worth noting that Rafael Obligado never set foot outside Argentina. The castle that was part of his and his wife's dreams came out of his imagination.

Rafael's son Carlos, also a poet, inherited El Castillo and celebrated various aspects of the life he knew there in his book *El poema del Castillo*. In 1951 the estancia passed into the hands of Carlos's eldest son, Héctor Rafael Obligado, whose brothers and sisters shared the family's other properties. La Independencia belongs to a different branch of the founder's descendants, the Davel Obligados.

The interiors of these two estancias, with their old photographs, paintings by well-known artists, inscribed books, and ornamental oddments—some the relics of history—reflect an atmosphere of cultural refinement combined with a love of the land. Oaks, palms, and cedars of Lebanon are to be found in the park, as well as native species like the jacaranda, the *palo borracho*, and the *ceibo*.

Left: The library's cedar shelves hold French, Spanish, and Argentine literature dating back to the eighteenth century. The stone balls are the missiles of the famed Argentine bolas.

Right: A tortoiseshell comb inscribed "Death to the French; let the world know that a great Rosas exists." Often caricatured in lithographs of the day, such outrageously large combs—some over three feet across— were unique to Argentina. Worn by upper- class women, they frequently bore political slogans proclaiming the wearer's allegiance to Rosas. This one, the work of the famous artisan Masculino, once belonged to the wife of the legendary caudillo Facundo Quiroga.

Below: El Castillo's dining room features this carved eighteenth-century chestnut chest from Castile. The copper untensils are from the last century.

La Segunda

La Segunda, having twice celebrated centennials, is one of the oldest establishments in Buenos Aires Province. It stands on the shores of the Laguna de la Viuda, a lake eighty-five or so miles south of the Argentine capital.

The history of the place begins toward the end of the eighteenth century, when the viceroys of the Río de la Plata were trying to put an end to smuggling and to the clandestine slaughter of wild cattle. At the same time, to secure the southern frontier against Indian attacks, it became necessary to encourage people scattered on the plain to live in settlements, such as that of San Juan Bautista de Chascomús, which was founded in 1779. Pioneer ranchers in this territory received land in exchange for guaranteeing to build a house on it and to raise cattle. It was in this way that Juan Rodríguez, a captain of the king's army, was granted permission to settle close to Chascomús and the Salado River. Proof of his determination was the presence of his wife, Luisa Tadea Martínez, who accompanied him in the enterprise.

Left: Gauchos once sipped maté mornings and evenings sitting in this inglenook fireplace, where a kettle was always kept on the boil. The refreshing drink is brewed from the leaf and tender stems of Ilex paraguayensis.

Right: A shed with old farm wagons and implements.

Left: Adapted for modern use, a carriage lamp becomes an elegant adornment on the whitened brick wall of the long porch.

Right: These massive masonry piers at the gateway to the park date from about 1790. In the colonial style, they may be the oldest surviving example of rural architecture anywhere on the pampa.

Below: La Segunda's facade is a perfect example of the vernacular style of the early estancia. Its simple lines are well suited to the flatness of the immense plains.

Nothing seemed more fitting than that a soldier should inhabit this dangerous region. But what was remarkable was that after Rodríguez's premature death his widow became the heart and soul of the establishment, ruling over its affairs with authority, wisdom, and courage. Such was the woman's fame that in tribute to her the shallow lake near the main house became known as "the Widow's lagoon."

Her daughter Ursula, who married a Spaniard, Mariano Fernández, inherited the land, cattle, horses, the hundreds of trees planted by her family, the buildings, and that admirable symbol of the decision to settle the place—the solid masonry gate piers that mark the entrance to the estancia's park. Built around 1790, they are perhaps the oldest example of rural architecture anywhere on the pampa.

Thanks to the law of emphyteusis laid down in the 1820s, land adjoining the estancia could be rented from the government and eventually purchased. Thus the estate grew to contain close to seventy square miles, and its boundaries reached the Salado. This was when the main house was built.

La Segunda acquired its present name in 1848, when it was bought by one of the great ranchers of the area, General Prudencio Ortiz de Rozas, another brother of Juan Manuel de Rosas. It fell to Prudencio to put down a rebellion of ranchers

in the south of the province and to cut its leaders' throats. As he already owned another property in the area, La Primera, the general gave his second establishment, on the Laguna de la Viuda, its simple numerical name, La Segunda. He paid almost half a million pesos for it, part in cash, part in houses he owned in Buenos Aires. But his ownership lasted only a short time. In 1853, the year after his brother's downfall, he chose to go and live in Europe, and the property passed into the hands of Enrique Ochoa, a wealthy impresario of beef-salting plants.

To transport his cattle more easily into Buenos Aires, Ochoa built a bridge, the Puente Alsina, over the Riachuelo, on the southern edge of the city, naming it after his friend, the governor of the province. But Ochoa never shared the enthusiasm of neighboring ranchers for advancing money to sheepshearers so as to secure a supply of labor, always a scarce commodity in the thinly populated province. When Ochoa died in 1873, his son-in-law Juan Acebal bought the estate from the heirs and gave it to his wife, Emilia, as a birthday present. It was an extraordinary gift, especially since a prosperous period lay just ahead for Argentine estancias. Refrigeration had just been invented, opening a vast market for the exportation of frozen meat. Under the management of Juan Acebal and his son, Juan Acebal Ochoa, La Segunda underwent a series of improvements. The land was fenced off in the 1880s, when fifteen sections were enclosed and each was given the name of a saint. There were fine flocks of sheep and a herd of purebred shorthorns, looked after mainly by Basque hands, for around 1860 this part of the province was almost repopulated by immigrants from both sides of the Pyrenees.

The main house, with its simple lines and veranda supported by slender iron posts,

Above: A glazed tile plaque chronicles La Segunda's fortunes. The establishment dates from 1785.

Below: The tiny chapel survives a tangle of vegetation.

An ancient maze of boxwood overlooks the shallow lake named for the formidable widow who first ran the estancia. Such lakes, or lagunas, are rich in waterfowl. Argentina boasts close to a thousand different species of birds.

is the same one that stands today. Only slightly remodeled, it retains the charms of the past, when it once was visited by Argentine president Carlos Pellegrini, who spent a few days at La Segunda shortly after ending his term of office.

When Juan Acebal Ochoa died childless in 1934, the estate passed into the hands of his nieces and nephews. Liliana Acebal de Soto inherited the house, which afterward came into the hands of her son, the architect Roberto Soto Acebal, the father of Carmen and Luciana, the present owners. They speak of the estancia as their "country place," for, owing to the numerous successions, the surrounding land has been reduced to just under 250 acres and produces a scant income. They look after the buildings themselves and live in harmony with the generous spirits that inhabit the main house, opening and closing doors, taking out blankets, and refusing to abandon the place, however much exorcism is employed.

The estancia also has a boathouse—before the lake became choked with reeds it was possible to row on it—a chapel, and sheds that hold a collection of old wagons and carriages. Amid hundred-year-old trees are garden paths edged with boxwood, and there are also three pomegranate shrubs that may have been planted by Captain Rodríguez and doña Tadea. The park boasts *paraísos*, eucalyptuses, oaks, elms, ashes, and camphor trees, while all around is an almost impenetrable wood that provides cover and protection for wildlife.

Los Yngleses

Los Yngleses lies nearly two hundred miles southeast of Buenos Aires on the Tuyú coast where the broad River Plate estuary meets the sea. The place was visited in the mid-eighteenth century by Thomas Falkner, an English slave-ship doctor who in 1732 became a Jesuit priest. *Tuyú*, in the language of the local Indians, meant "mud" or "clay," explained Falkner in his celebrated account *Description of Patagonia, and the adjoining parts of South America. . . .* Published in Hereford in 1774, his book describes the remote area around Cape San Antonio, where the land forms a peninsula with shallow lakelets and marshy ground in which crabs bred and the woodlands were dense with such native trees as the *tala*, the *coronilla*, and the *sombra de toro*. Indian hunters combed this backwater for the wild horses that found refuge there.

Some forty years on, when the country was no longer part of the Spanish Empire, Esteban Márquez, an Argentine-born landowner, settled the Rincón del Tuyú, south of the Salado River, which then marked the frontier with the Indians. He named his establishment El Carmen and put up its first rough buildings. Later, the property

Left: A corner of the living room features an English organ, on which is displayed a gleaming set of copperware presented to the owner's mother on the occasion of her wedding in 1925. On the wall are water-color landscapes by Thomas Gibson. The furniture in the dining room beyond is seventeenth-century English. Over the mantel is a painting of four employees of the establishment by B. S. Donaldson.

Right: Mementoes of Los Yngleses's past—old photographs, documents, and medals—decorate the walls of the comfortable, unashamedly old-fashioned office.

passed into the hands of John Gibson, a son of the founder of a firm of Glasgow textile merchants, who came to Buenos Aires in 1818, hoping to profit from the economic advantages offered by the newly emancipated South American republics. He wanted to export hides and other local products but noted that Buenos Aires's richest traders were also sheep and cattle breeders. Receiving his father's permission to buy and stock lands in the province of Buenos Aires, Gibson soon came to own dozens of leagues and thousands of head of cattle. In time, the area became Argentina's first Scottish settlement.

Thomas, the younger of the Gibsons, reached Argentina in 1837 with an engineering diploma under his arm and with great enthusiasm for El Carmen. By then the place was known as Los Yngleses—The Englishmen—despite its owners' Scottish origins. To reach the estancia from the capital in those days, Gibson traveled to Chascomús by diligence, stopping over at the estancia of Ricardo Newton, who became famous for having introduced the first wire fencing into the country in 1846. Continuing on horse, Gibson had then to ride some fifteen leagues a day to the estate. By the river route, on the Salado and Tuyú, one was at the whim of favorable winds.

The Gibsons fell in love with raw nature, and the estate's mysterious wilds proved an oasis of peace in the midst of endless civil war. In letters still in the family's possession, the Gibsons told their Glasgow relatives about the beauty of the land and how they enjoyed riding a horse as it swam through lagoons among whose rushes herons and spoonbills made their nests.

Thomas's taste for nature, which inspired him to paint pictures of the landscape, did not conflict with his excellent administration of the family's farming interests. A wise manager in difficult times, he succeeded in eluding the French blockade in 1838 and the Anglo-French blockade seven years later. In 1839 the survivors of the rebellion of estancia owners from the south of the province, whom the tyrant Rosas had stiffly punished, made good their escape via the port of Tuyú. Owing to the war—at the time, Rosas was also intervening in the chaotic political life of Uruguay—the estancia was short of hands, and, with their husbands absent, the women took over the work, including shearing, the profitable activity that the establishment had recently introduced.

Expert by now in adapting to local conditions, the Gibsons became pioneers in sheep farming and, after experimentation, found that the Lincoln breed was best suited to the area. In time, they imported the first machine of its kind to bale wool and a dip that combated sheep ticks. Ultimately, they established direct commercial links between the port of Tuyú and British markets. Their flocks were tended by Irish and Scottish shepherds who came specially to Argentina and whose descendants, with names like Taylor, Poe, and Cummings, still work in the locality.

Los Yngleses had to cede part of its 108 square miles for the founding of General Lavalle, the district's chief town. With recent profits, the main house was extensively rebuilt in 1872, and its new Scottish-style roof became the model for sheep-breeding establishments. The farmhands' house and kitchen, the wool sheds, and the tallow works formed a circle around a grass courtyard, a layout whose origin may have been defensive.

After Thomas's death in 1902, the property passed to Ernesto, who inherited the estancia's buildings and nearly twenty-two square miles of surrounding land. An amateur ornithologist, he was a friend and correspondent of the writer and naturalist W. H. Hudson, with whom he exchanged information about the region's rich variety of birds, particularly waders and waterfowl.

PAGES 52–53

Left: Corbie gables, a feature of Scottish architecture, were introduced in 1872, when the main house was rebuilt. Despite the fact that the Gibsons were Scots, the estancia was called Los Yngleses, The Englishmen.

Right: More than colorful ornaments, the red buckets hang in readiness for putting out possible fires.

Once important for breeding sheep, the estancia now has a herd of purebred native longhorn cattle. The first cows were introduced into Argentina in 1555, and in time they created the country's great wealth.

Above: Farmhands drinking maté. The vessel from which the beverage is sipped, also called a maté, is most commonly a pear-shaped gourd. It can be ornamented with silver, decorated with carving, or even clad in a bull's scrotum. Elaborate matés are fashioned entirely of silver. The one here is of horn.

Right: The Gibsons imported this machine for baling wool, the first of its kind in Argentina. Los Yngleses gave rise to the country's earliest Scottish settlement.

Los Yngleses suffered in the economic depression of the 1930s. By then Ernesto had died, and his widow rented out the estate. It fell to Francisco Boote, who married a Gibson, to reverse the decline and restock the establishment, which had come into his hands without cattle. His children, John (who married Elisa Magrane), Rosemary Boote de Cavanagh, and Elizabeth Boote de Gurmendi are the estancia's present owners. John resides permanently on the premises, something uncommon among Argentine ranchers. As sheep are no longer profitable, the flocks of Lincolns are little more than a memory. Today's Aberdeen Angus are tended on horseback, the only way to traverse the swampy pastures. The estate also takes pride in its herd of purebred native cattle, which have once more become a valuable commodity.

Among its memorabilia, Los Yngleses still preserves the medicine chest of an English ship sunk around 1880 off Cape San Antonio. In this box is an unnerving blue bottle of pure poison—an elixir of vitriol. The captain of the ill-fated ship accepted the estancia's hospitality and is buried in the local cemetery. The estate's lookout tower was built out of the timbers of his ship.

La Vigía

La Vigía is located in one of the most fertile parts of the Argentine, the rolling pampa in the northwest of Buenos Aires Province, an area that at the end of the last century turned from livestock production to growing great quantities of wheat and maize for export.

Currently the property of Javier Garcia del Solar and Fernando del Solar Dorrego, La Vigía's main house—with its dry moat, iron-grilled windows, cannon, and roof battlements—still resembles a small fort. It serves as a reminder of the Indian raids that ravaged the region until late into the nineteenth century. Only some fifteen years ago, a cellar was discovered in which the settlers used to hide in the event of a siege. It contained newspapers from the 1870s, the final years of frontier conflict.

The founder of the estancia was Luis Dorrego, the son of a Portuguese nobleman, Domingo Dorrego, who came to Buenos Aires, where he married María Asunción Salas. The couple's other son, Manuel, fought in the army of independence and rose to the rank of colonel. As a politican and journalist he laid the foundations of doctrinaire Federalism and in 1827–28 served as governor of Buenos Aires Province. This period marked the beginning of the complicated civil war between the Unitarians and Federals, which led to Manuel's tragic death (he was executed by a firing squad under orders of the Unitarian General Lavalle) and ushered Rosas to power.

Luis, meanwhile, had devoted himself to commerce. In 1815, in partnership with

Left: Flanking the entrance to La Vigía's main house are marble busts of Manuel Dorrego and Luis Dorrego Indart, brother and son, respectively, of the estancia's founder. Manuel and his brother Luis met tragic ends as a result of civil feuds that racked Argentine life for decades after independence from Spain.

Right: Built around 1820, the blocklike house, with its iron-grilled windows and roof battlements, resembles a small fort.

Above: The hut where Manuel Dorrego, the deposed governor of Buenos Aires Province, found temporary refuge from his pursuers. His execution in 1828 was a turning point in the country's history and unleashed a long and gory civil war.

Right: A shepherd on horseback drives his flock homeward.

*Left: A gilded mirror and silver tea service
add a rich glow to the dining room.*

*Below: The living room's high ceiling helps
keep it cool in the sultry Argentine summer.
The formerly gaslit chandelier once adorned
the family's mansion in Buenos Aires.*

Rosas and Juan Nepomuceno Terrero, he founded one of the country's first beef-salting plants. Later, at a date that his descendants cannot pinpoint, he settled land that had no formal owners in the present districts of Rojas and Salto, to the west of Buenos Aires. When the provincial government offered grants under the law of emphyteusis, he rented almost two hundred square miles in the district of 25 de Mayo, not far from a holding that he had already settled. On his nearly three hundred square miles of property he carved out several estancias, among them La Vigía—The Watchman, or Lookout—which is associated with the last days of his brother, Manuel, who sought refuge there after his defeat by Lavalle and before he was captured.

Coming into conflict in the 1830s with his old partner Governor Rosas, Luis was forced into exile in São Paulo, where he died in poverty because there was no way of remitting funds to him. But his fortune in land, together with his real estate in Buenos Aires—twenty-five properties on Calle Florida, the most important street in Buenos Aires, alone—made his widow, Inés Indart, one of the province's richest women. Their children—Luis, Angela, Magdalena, and Felisa—also figured among the wealthiest people of their day.

Luis, who married Enriqueta Lezica Aldao, inherited La Vigía, which he visited frequently. The journey was made by stagecoach and required changing horses in

An old map of Buenos Aires Province adorns the office walls. Argentina's richest province is also its second largest.

An old map of Buenos Aires Province adorns the office walls. Argentina's richest province is also its second largest.

Luján, Areco, and Salto. Enriqueta's black servant would climb to the top of the mirador and, spying the dust trail from the masters' diligence, know when to put on the meat to barbecue. Luis died at the estancia in 1871, a victim of cholera, which he had contracted in the city.

Life at La Vigía was too Spartan for his widow, who preferred the comforts of their villa on the outskirts of Buenos Aires. On one of her many trips to Europe she brought back a manager named Philip Hughes, whom she hired to modernize the estancia's methods, which until then had been run along the old lines, with native cattle and few crops. Hughes not only carried out the task but also grew rich buying land on the border with Santa Fe Province.

Inés Dorrego, wife of multimillionaire Saturnino Unzué, was La Vigía's next owner. Although she visited the estate only once a year, she kept it in good condition, adding modern bathrooms around the beginning of the century. The Unzués had chosen to build a deluxe mansion at another of their estancias, and this accounts for the fact that La Vigía never lost its native character. Inés died without a direct heir, but wanting the estate to stay in the Dorrego family she left the house and some 1,700 acres to her grandnieces and -nephews.

The house was built around 1820; later, a wing was added to one side of the courtyard. The new wrought-iron window grills here are more ornate than the earlier ones. A wooden door opens onto this courtyard, which shelters a wellhead and orange and lemon trees. The present owner has placed marble busts of Manuel Dorrego and Luis Dorrego Indart on the veranda.

The interiors contain furniture and art objects from other of the family's residences,

such as the Miró palace, an obligatory point of reference in the Buenos Aires of 1890. One of the house's most beautiful adornments is the large gaslit chandelier from a former Dorrego salon in Buenos Aires.

The farmhands' kitchen is famous in the area. On holidays, neighbors would drive there in sulkies or ride in on horseback to listen to the improvised singing contests of gaucho bards, who accompanied themselves on the guitar. Some of their themes concerned the history of La Vigía, for a popular poetry had grown up thereabouts dealing with the death of Colonel Dorrego.

Not far from the kitchen, the so-called historic hut stands witness to the last days of the governor who had found refuge at La Vigía before he was taken to Navarro for execution. In Argentina—and this appears time and again in tales of the countryside—there is an intimate connection between the idea of sanctuary and the word *estancia*.

Malal-Hué en Chapadmalal

Malal-Hué en Chapadmalal (originally Chapadmalal), near Mar del Plata and six miles from the Atlantic coast in the district of Chapadmalal, was Indian land in 1854, when it became the property of the Martínez de Hoz family. In the Araucanian language, the estancia's name means "in the muddy (or boggy) corral." As this area is full of streams that run into the sea, the descriptive designation is not unlike that of *rincón*. The estate, distinguished for its vine-clad main house in the style of a Scottish castle, was once famed for the cattle and racehorses it bred. Today the green, rolling land with its rich black soil (said to be among the best arable land in the world) is used almost exclusively for agriculture. Wheat, potatoes, oats, barley, and rye have been grown here since the beginning of the century, and in recent years sunflowers, maize, and soya.

At the end of the eighteenth century, José Alfredo Martínez de Hoz, a childless Buenos Aires merchant and city councillor, sent to Spain for his nephew, Narciso Alonso de Armiño. As a sign of gratitude for being taken into his uncle's firm, the

Left: The Martínez de Hoz family's coat of arms, behind which are embedded some fragments of a nearby old Spanish fort. The autumn-tinted Virginia creeper makes a good foil for the gray stone bench, whose sphinx plinths and other neoclassical elements epitomize the great attraction that European culture has held for Argentine cattlemen.

Right: A Scottish castle built by an English architect in 1906 on a remote South American plain is a succinct illustration of one side of the deep-seated Argentine conflict between looking inward to native American values and outward to those of Europe.

young man adopted his benefactor's surname, thus becoming a kind of second founder of the family in the region of the River Plate. Dedicating his life to commerce and banking, Narciso came to own estancias in the districts of Cañuelas and Castelli. In the 1820s he involved himself in President Bernardino Rivadavia's scheme for developing the hinterland by the distribution of vast allotments for a yearly rental fee. (Later, under Rosas, this system lapsed.) As a result, his elder son, José T. Martínez de Hoz, eventually bought nearly two hundred square miles of land between Cape Corrientes and the River Quequén Grande in the southeast of Buenos Aires Province. At the time, Indian raids still plagued the region. To thwart the attacks, another of Narciso's sons, Colonel Miguel Martínez de Hoz, who died in the 1865–70 war between Argentina and Paraguay, fortified the estancia with iron casemates.

José, a cofounder in 1866 of the Argentine Rural Society, an elite cattleman's club that holds an annual livestock show in the Palermo section of Buenos Aires, died young in 1871, before the boom in cattle that came with the invention of refrigeration and with the systematic decimation of the Indians. His widow sent her sons Miguel Alfredo and Eduardo to be educated in England.

When Miguel Alfredo came of age, he chose to return home to take charge of his inheritance. Selling the Castelli land, which by then was rather depleted, he kept the estate at Chapadmalal. It contained some 115 square miles, to which he added other properties.

In 1890, as a sign of his confidence in the future of the estate, he built the first of several sheds, divided the land into fenced sections, and brought in pedigreed shorthorn cattle, shire horses, and Lincoln sheep. At the age of twenty-two, he set out to provide his establishment with the latest improvements in breeding techniques then being tried out in England.

Chapadmalal's sumptuous manorial house was begun in 1906, the work of an English architect, Walter B. Basset-Smith, who designed a number of other important rural houses in addition to summer homes in Mar del Plata. The mansion's warm interiors are adorned with oak furniture, and its neo-Gothic chapel is decorated with carvings brought from Europe. The park, in an area where the only native species is the *currú*, a thorny shrub, is planted with introduced species such as oaks, Indian chestnuts, ashes, cedars, firs, beeches, and plane trees. Under the careful eye of Miguel Alfredo's wife, Julia Elena Acevedo, the garden had a section dedicated wholly to roses and another, in the Italian style, containing only two colors of flower, as well as examples of the art of topiary.

English racing saddles hang in the tack room. The first horses—seventy-two in number—reached Argentina in 1536.

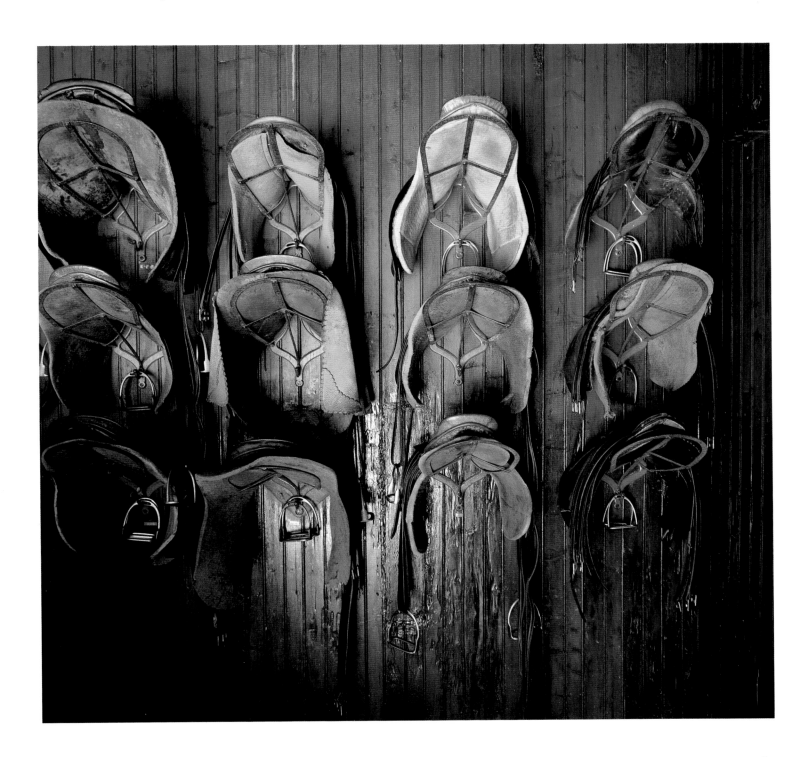

Left: A file of eucalyptuses, a species adapted to a wide variety of climatic conditions, serves both as a windbreak and for firewood. An Australian tree, its seeds were first distributed among Buenos Aires ranchers in 1858 by Domingo F. Sarmiento.

Right: The gravestone of the champion Thoroughbred Botafogo.

Below: An old photograph showing José Alfredo Martínez de Hoz with a stablehand and one of his racehorses.

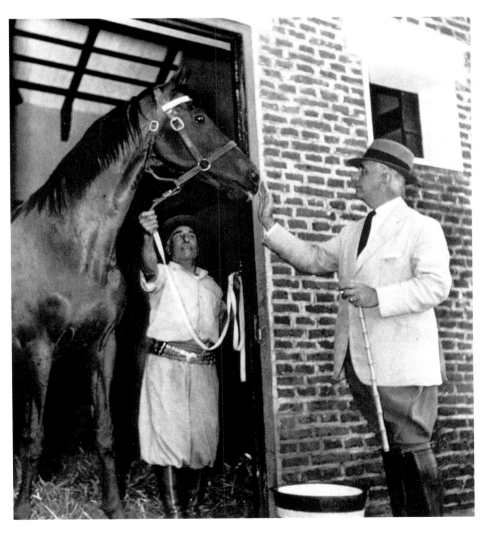

The estancia's photo album charts a series of improvements in the early years of this century. Stables were added, as were a shearing shed, corrals, a huge vat for dipping cattle, a blacksmith's forge, and a house for the farmhands. At the time, the establishment's great pride was its purebred hackney horses, which were excellent trotters. In fact, Miguel Alfredo went to London in 1907 to show some eighty of his hackneys, for which he won prizes and championships. He even entered fashionable competitions, one of which involved driving a carriage twice weekly between London and Guildford. In 1909, after a run from Hampton Court to Olympia, he found that his rival was a fellow enthusiast, the American millionaire Alfred Vanderbilt.

Around 1913, as the automobile began to displace draft animals, Miguel Alfredo was persuaded to start up a stud farm for Thoroughbreds, using his own mares as its basis. As a champion sire was essential to such an enterprise, Martínez de Hoz traveled to London, where he paid £30,000 for Craganour, a horse belonging to the king. The animal would have won that year's Derby but was disqualified owing to

Miguel Alfredo Martínez de Hoz, who once competed in a coach race against Alfred Vanderbilt. The portrait is by the Italian painter Giovanni Boldini.

Right: In 1909 Miguel Alfredo Martínez de Hoz won a famous coach race from Hampton Court to Olympia with his Argentine horses.

Below: A sampling of the cups won by the family's racing stable.

the disturbance caused in the race when in an act of protest a militant suffragette threw herself under his hooves.

A slump in the livestock market in 1923 and again in 1930 struck hard at the family fortune. As Miguel Alfredo had been taken ill—he died in 1935—his son José Alfredo took over the estate in partnership with his brother and sister, Miguel Alfredo and María Julia. In order to save Chapadmalal, half the land was sold off, and a strip along the coast was set aside for house lots in the beach resort that bears the estancia's name. José Alfredo's activity went beyond his own farm. In the 1940s he presided over the Argentine Rural Society during the first government of Juan Perón, a period that proved hard for large landowners.

In 1959 Chapadmalal was divided between the two branches of the family. Forming a private company, José Alfredo and his children, José Alfredo, Juan Miguel, Ana Helena Martínez de Hoz de Torres Zavaleta, and Carola Martínez de Hoz de Ramos Mexía—the present owners—kept the main house of the old estate and gave it its current name. The stud farm was closed in 1986.

San Ramón

San Ramón, beyond San Antonio de Areco, eighty miles northwest of Buenos Aires, not only keeps alive the memory of Irish immigration to the Argentine pampa but at the same time is proud of its cattle-breeding record, for the estancia has provided the annual livestock show in Palermo with dozens of great champions.

Located on highish land good for both farming and grazing, the property was bought in 1864 by Michael Duggan, a thirty-five-year-old Irishman who had arrived in Argentina in 1859, accompanied by his younger brothers, Thomas and Daniel. They had owned a farm in Mullingham, County Longford, but like so many of their fellow countrymen who left the old sod in search of a better life they reached Buenos Aires with only a few shillings in their pockets.

The Duggans, who had no relatives in Argentina, became friends of Father Anthony Fahy, the spiritual leader of the local Irish community. This venerable priest was well known as a matchmaker, and he married Thomas to Marcela Casey, the daughter of an Irish rancher who had amassed considerable wealth. The three brothers—though two remained bachelors—set up in business together breeding sheep, something that immigrants from the British Isles were particularly good at.

Left: A prize Hereford bull. Three Duggan brothers came from Ireland in 1859 and by 1890 figured among the top landowners of Buenos Aires Province. The first Herefords reached Argentina in 1862.

Right: A barn at San Ramón, Thomas Duggan's favorite estancia among the twenty-eight he owned.

San Ramón's seventeen-odd square miles became the first step on their way to a fortune. The land was suitable for sheep and cheaper than property along the Salado River, which had long since been divided among Argentine and English ranchers. Carefully managed sheep multiplied prodigiously. The Duggans became wool-shipping agents, they promoted the arrival of Irish shepherds, and all the while they kept buying land in districts recently conquered from the Indians. By 1890 they figured in the top rank of landowners in Buenos Aires Province, with property in such far-flung localities as San Antonio de Areco, Arrecifes, Giles, Navarro, Chacabuco, Salto, General Villegas, and General Arenales.

Thomas's brother-in-law, Eduardo Casey, brought the Duggans into the booming construction trade. Casey's group was involved in erecting a gigantic wholesale fruit market on the south side of Buenos Aires and had another large building scheme afoot in Montevideo when the depression of 1890 set in. In the ensuing collapse, the Duggans lost at least one of their great estancias. But they steadily recovered. At the turn of the century, Thomas, who had inherited his brothers' wealth, owned nearly twelve hundred square miles of land, which was divided into twenty-eight estancias. San Ramón was his favorite among them, and he spent more time in the country than did the majority of Argentine cattlemen, who tended to live in Buenos Aires.

At one point, when he bought a fine herd of shorthorns from their Scottish owner, the presence of so many similar red cows at San Ramón astonished all the estate's neighbors. Even the former owner, who judged one or two shows at Palermo, said that he should never have let such champion stock leave Britain. Their original name, Syttithon, was kept. Thomas Duggan succeeded where many Irish-Argentines in the

Left: The classically inspired statues that overlook the pool add a humanizing note to the infinite landscape, while the avenue of eucalyptus trees gives off a delicious medicinal scent.

Below: The main house, English-inspired and with a number of fussy Victorian details, has more in common with the kind of domestic architecture found in the warmer reaches of the British Commonwealth than with Argentina. This is also true of the trim lawn and flower beds and the neat red-pebbled paths.

district failed, clinging to sheep-breeding after it had declined as a sound business.
Herefords were also raised at San Ramón.

To the end of his life, Thomas was a fervent Irish nationalist. It was even hinted
that he had left Ireland for political reasons. Loyal to his convictions, he never dealt
with English meat-packing firms or with the Bank of London. His descendants
suspect that he financed the anti-British revolutionary movement. Sir Roger Casement,
hanged in Ireland as a result of the 1916 Easter uprising, had, according to one old
photograph, spent some days at San Ramón in 1908.

On Thomas's death, his sons, Carlos, Eduardo, and Bernardo, inherited their
father's properties, which they incorporated as Duggan Brothers. San Ramón formed
part of the concern, and its magnificent herds produced twenty-eight grand champions
at Palermo. On three occasions—in 1943, 1956, and 1957—the brothers achieved
the great feat of obtaining maximum distinctions with different breeds simultaneously.

Luisa Duggan de Martín y Herrera, the daughter of Bernardo and granddaughter
of Thomas, is San Ramón's present owner. When she was born in 1930 her father
nearly named her Syttithon, such was his enthusiasm for the successes of his purebred
stock. In those years, the farm work was done with draft horses, and some fifteen
hundred shire horses were needed for pulling plows. Mechanization began in the
1940s, with iron-wheeled tractors. Meanwhile, the makeup of the rural population
began to change. Through intermarriage the Irish have so assimilated into Argentine
life that few of them any longer speak English.

Shorthorn breeding was phased out in 1987, but Herefords, both horned
and polled, are still raised. San Ramón's most recent grand champion took the
prize in 1990.

The estancia's main house is simple and trim. It has a small veranda and is
surrounded by paths of reddish pebbles. Like the houses of other great Irish estancias,
it has grown according to the growth of the family. The large dining room is hung
with portraits of the Duggans. In honor of one of the founders of a legendary Irish-
Argentine family, Marcela Casey's portrait has pride of place above the living room
fireplace.

Huetel

Huetel is one of the pampa's most luxurious estancias. Of unmistakable Louis XIII style, the main house rises in stately grandeur and is so placed in the treeless expanse of its natural grassland setting as to present a dramatic contrast with the densely planted park through which the mansion is approached.

The heart of a typical nineteenth-century estancia—what Argentines refer to as the *casco*—consisted of the main residence, in which either the estate manager lived or the proprietor's family in summer, together with thatched adobe huts, or *ranchos*, for the foremen and hired hands. There were also outbuildings that served as kitchens and warehouses for tools, hides, tallow, and riding gear. The *casco* included corrals for branding and for the work horses. Before the advent of wire fencing in the 1860s, many of these old *cascos* were ringed by dry moats as much as twelve feet deep and twenty-five feet wide. Such ditches not only served as a defense against Indian depradations but also protected orchards, vegetable patches, and breeding stock.

Left: This château in the style of Louis XIII and its thousand-acre park are located not outside Paris but within two hundred miles of Buenos Aires. Argentine wealth was such at the turn of the century that cattlemen could freely indulge their fancies in creating their ideal homes.

Right: In the evening glow, the tiled porch and its delicate ironwork harmonize with the nearby foliage. The parks of some estancias amounted to arboretums; Huetel's once contained 400,000 trees.

As an estancia prospered, its owners might add a wing to the old residence or erect an opulent new house away from the old *casco*. A chapel might also be built, or rebuilt, in the park.

Huetel is a classic estancia and a true monument to the idea of country life as held by Argentina's great ranchers at the turn of the century. The establishment, 250-odd square miles of land in the district of 25 de Mayo, allowed its owner, Concepción Unzué de Casares, to give free rein to her fancy in transforming this piece of pampa into a painstaking copy of a French château from the reign of the Bourbons. The wild magnificence of the solitary plain was by then but a memory, and mansions like Huetel were built to prove the fact.

The elegant design of this gateway, with its cattle grid, is repeated in other estancias belonging to the Unzué family.

Huetel's own train station. The Prince of Wales once spent a night here in his sleeping car.

At the same time, Huetel—"armadillo" in the language of the Indians—attested to the success of the Unzué family, which in three generations had become one of the richest in Argentina. Francisco, the founder of the River Plate branch of the Unzués, had been a merchant and high-ranking official in Buenos Aires at the end of the eighteenth century. His eldest son, Saturnino, acquired land and owned fruit warehouses; on his death in 1854 he left a considerable legacy. But it was Saturnino E., a member of the third generation, who gave the family's affairs a decisive turn. He owned ranches, shipped wool, and was a private banker and skilled land speculator. He also financed the 1874 revolution headed by ex-president Bartolomé Mitre. The unsuccessful coup—a protest over which candidate would succeed Sarmiento as president—reached its culmination in the battle of La Verde, which was fought on land that forms part of Huetel. In this conflict, Colonel Francisco Borges, who commanded a brigade under Mitre, committed suicide when he saw that he had backed the wrong side. Making a target of himself, he rode his horse toward enemy lines and took two bullets in the stomach. His grandson, the poet Jorge Luis Borges, in one of three poems commemorating his ancestor's death, wrote of this episode:

> *On the 26th of November 1874,*
> *so that death might take you in its eye,*

Distinguished guests were often asked to plant a tree. In 1925 the Prince of Wales, later to become Edward VIII, performed the service.

Left: An elaborate fountain mirrors the elegant château of an estate named for one of Argentina's humblest creatures, the armadillo.

Below: This splendid dovecote provided table fare. In a country where you could kill a cow for a steak and go unpunished as long as you left the hide, squab was a delicacy.

you wrapped yourself in a white poncho and rode out on a silver-colored horse.

The colonel died of his wounds two days later in a room in one of the estancia's older buildings.

When Saturnino E. died in 1886, he left a legacy of gold, stock shares, urban lots, and hundreds and hundreds of square miles of pampa. Concepción, his younger daughter and the wife of Carlos Casares, thus became an extremely wealthy woman and decided to turn the estate into one of the finest houses in the province.

Located some two hundred miles to the southwest of the capital, Huetel stands on property acquired by her forebears around 1860. In 1889 Concepción and Carlos began to lay out the park, for which they set aside close to one thousand acres, an exceptional amount of land even by the standards of the time, when the woodlands of the great establishments were vast. The plan of the grounds was the work of German engineer and landscape gardener G. Welther. (The park was later redesigned by Carlos Thays III.) Four hundred thousand trees were planted, a third of them evergreen; the saplings were shipped by train from nurseries in Buenos Aires to the town of 9 de Julio, and from there by cart to the estancia. The first young trees were devoured by locusts, a plague that was not eradicated until the 1940s, but eventually the plantation grew into a magnificent park. It contains, among other species, cedars, planes, oaks, pines, eucalyptuses, and a number of superb magnolias.

Construction of the house began in 1906 under the supervision of the architect J. Dunant, but Carlos Casares did not live to see the mansion finished. He died in 1907, two years before it was ready for habitation. The result is an elegant three-story building with marble staircases, a generous veranda, balconies on the second floor, and a slate-gray mansard roof. The rooms number in the dozens, including great wainscoted salons, and the furniture is of different styles, all European. The park also contains a neo-Gothic chapel, white-pebbled drives, fountains, statues, and a lake.

Huetel should have provided the perfect setting for an active social life, but Concepción Unzué was reserved and had a mind of her own. Keeping an eye on the

Left: Aberdeen Angus, a favorite breed of Buenos Aires cattlemen, scamper across the outstretched plain. Pampa is the Quechua word for this open space, this vast grassland, which has inspired generations of Argentine poets and writers.

Right: The pleasant dairy, appropriately in white with hints of blue, where guests are invited for a glass of fresh milk.

progress of the garden, she drove about in a pony trap to oversee the smallest details. A devout woman, she aided the community with gifts of schools, hospices, and hospitals.

In 1925 the Prince of Wales, who was to become Edward VIII, paid the estancia a short visit, arriving at the estate's own railway station on its own branch line. The story runs that, exhausted by the official duties of his visit to Argentina, the prince allowed himself the luxury of sleeping late in his rail car, thereby skipping the local festivities arranged in his honor. That night, however, he was treated to an extraordinary tango spectacle. The legendary Carlos Gardel-José Razzano duo had been specially brought in for the princely soirée. As it was a men-only affair, Concepción herself was not present.

Doña Concepción died in 1959, aged nearly one hundred. Childless, she left the estancia to a niece, Josefina Alzaga Unzué de Sánchez Elía. Her daughter, Josefina Sánchez Alzaga de Larreta, is Huetel's present owner. She holds some 27 square miles (about 17,000 acres); an equal amount, which belonged to her brother Horacio, is in the hands of María Elena Castellanos de Sánchez Alzaga and her sons, Carlos and Ignacio. The latter manages the estancia. The establishment has a herd of Aberdeen Angus and crops of soya, maize, and sunflowers.

La Peregrina

Two hundred and fifty miles south of Buenos Aires, on the highway between Balcarce and Mar del Plata, the monotony of the plain is relieved by a range of low hills, the Sierra de los Padres, named for the tireless Jesuit fathers who once traveled the length and breadth of the area in a fruitless attempt to settle it. In this picturesque setting, with views over woodlands and fields and a small river—the Vivoratá—that runs through the heart of the estancia, we find La Peregrina.

According to Yuyú Guzmán, a historian of the pampa, the first white men to live here were the workers of a beef-salting plant set up on the banks of the Vivoratá in the 1850s by José Coelho Meyrelles, a Portuguese impresario. The plant was soon abandoned, and an estancia was formed from its assorted huts. The piece of land on which La Peregrina would later be built was first bought by Anacarsis Lanús. Later owners, the Imaz brothers, acquired more land, until one of them, Joaquín, ended up with the establishment's nearly fifty square miles. When he died at an early age, his widow, Petrona Hueguilar, took charge of the property.

In the 1880s the estate was fenced and divided into sections: "del Arbolito," "del Esquinero," "del Paraguayo," and "de San Bartolomé." Petrona had remarried; her second husband was Teófilo Bordeu. By the turn of the century, La Peregrina

Left: Four bays waiting to be saddled. In the Argentine, horses are exhaustively classified according to their coats and details of their markings. There are at least eleven different kinds of bays.

Right: A tropilla, *or little troop of horses, with its bell mare, crossing a bridge. "Every tropilla has a mare with a bell suspended from her neck," wrote William MacCann a hundred and fifty years ago, "and the horses, if well-trained, will never leave her side."*

Below: A pair of ombus tower over an old-style dwelling. No gaucho would sleep under the ombu, whose buttressed trunk can reach a circumference of over ninety feet. Much lore has grown up around this tree, which, in fact, is a shrub.

Right: "Your houses will be right when they match the windmill, which is an honest artifact," Le Corbusier told Argentines when he visited the country. Where natural boundaries are infrequent, water and wire fencing are indispensable elements for raising cattle.

Left: In the farmhands' kitchen a fire always burns. Maté and roast meat precede a morning's work.

Right: Like figures in a Millet painting, two men gathering potatoes loom out of the early morning mist.

Above: A Buenos Aires Province saddle, with the estancia's brand and the owner's initials worked in silver and gold. Saddle gear in the Argentine is far more elaborate than elsewhere. Until recently it was composed of so many layers and parts that it was said to have been a gaucho's bed by night and chest of drawers by day.

was a great estancia. Not only was cattle raised there but the estate was set in fields ideally suited to agriculture—especially potatoes.

A new house, set apart from the hubbub of the daily round of farmwork, was built in the Italianate style fashionable in Argentina's Belle Epoque. An elongated rectangular floor plan, wide verandas, marble staircases, classical columns, and a pink exterior that contrasted with the greenery of the park, all lent the place a serene beauty. Meanwhile, the original buildings, a typical old Argentine rural settlement—houses for the men who had worked at the salting factory, sheds, posts where horses were hitched or broken, fences, and huge ombus—were still there on the Vivoratá.

Between 1920 and 1959, Teófilo Vicente Bordeu became the driving force behind the establishment, managing it himself. He was particularly interested in rebuilding the old settlement, which he preferred to the great mansion erected by his mother. This represented a new outlook on the part of the landed class. The values of the past had been undergoing reconsideration, and the early buildings of the Argentine countryside—easily defendable single-story dwellings with broad verandas—began to be admired for their unique charm and for the sense of security that they generated. La Peregrina, which is today owned by the Bordeu children, presents a perfect example of the two facets of taste prevalent among proprietors of Argentine rural estates.

Arroyo Dulce
San Bartolo

These model establishments, divided by the Arroyo Dulce, a tributary of the Salto River, are located some 125 miles from the capital in the finest maize-producing area of western Buenos Aires Province. San Bartolo, which belongs to Carlos Green Devoto, is on one side of the stream, in the district of Rojas. On the other side, in Pergamino, stands the original *casco*, now called Arroyo Dulce ("sweetwater brook"), the property of Silvia Green.

In the period of the boom in wool, the estate was still one and was known as La Dulce. It was owned by Gregorio Lezama, who also had a villa in Buenos Aires on the present site of the Historical Museum in the park that bears his name. La Dulce then passed into the hands of another prosperous landowner, Roberto Cano, before it was bought by an Italian immigrant, Bartolomé Devoto.

Devoto had arrived in Argentina in 1851, at the age of seventeen, with his brother Antonio. Born in Lavagna, near Genoa, they began a modest new life working in

Left: Arroyo Dulce's main facade is an elaborate example of the Hispanic style, which enjoyed a revival among Argentine cattlemen in the 1920s. Here baroque embellishments contrast with overall austerity.

Right: The house is built around an elegantly arcaded central courtyard of Andalusian inspiration. The tiles and hanging lamp and the patio's central pool and fountain have their sources in southern Spain.

Left: In this modern utilitarian kitchen, natural wood fittings and copper utensils provide warmth and coziness.

Right: The varied collection of hats and tennis rackets on the cast-iron stand gives the hall a friendly air.

Below: The table and chairs, Spanish in style, are marked by massiveness and sobriety. Yet nothing in this large, carefully appointed dining room dominates the painting of La Boca, the old port of Buenos Aires, by the modern master Quinquela Martín.

Left: Shaded by Boston ivy, which the long, hot Argentine summers turn rich crimson and scarlet in autumn, this pergola—harboring an exquisite marble table—leads to the swimming pool.

Right: In a dramatic setting amid mature trees, the chapel is a fitting island of repose.

Below: Parthenocissus (Boston ivy) frames the view of the swimming pool, while a rampant bougainvillea has begun to embellish the pavilion's elegant geometrical lines.

a general goods store during the last years of the reign of Rosas. With their youth, innate thrift, unusual capacity for work, and sound business sense, the Devoto brothers made a rapid rise as partners in the property market. Buenos Aires was in the midst of a population explosion, and fortunes were made overnight. "Always buy up corner properties," was Bartolomé's guiding principle. And he acquired a number of these—at Lavalle and Reconquista, Viamonte and Leandro Alem, and other locations in the heart of downtown Buenos Aires. Later the brothers developed the residential neighborhood known as Villa Devoto, in the northwestern part of the city.

In time, the Devotos became one of the richest families in South America, an achievement all the more remarkable since their wealth was the fruit of their own labor, unlike many of the great Argentine fortunes, which had been handed down by early settlers. The brothers were founders of a long series of businesses that included banking, manufacturing and finance groups, and a match manufacturing company. Their acquisitions in rural areas began after they had amassed a fortune. They founded a town and leased out farmland in what is now the province of La Pampa to Italian, Spanish, and Croatian immigrants.

At the pinnacle of their success, however, disagreements between their wives caused the brothers to go their separate ways. Antonio, who had no children, retained a majority holding in the group; Bartolomé took the farming estates and the property businesses.

When Bartolomé died in Mar del Plata in 1920, his widow, Juana González, undertook to modernize the *casco* of La Dulce, renaming it San Bartolo in memory of her late husband. As even in periods of prosperity he had been thrifty in the

Above: Once the main house of an estancia called La Dulce, this simple single-story building, with its mirador, is presently used for San Bartolo's guests.

Left: San Bartolo's cellar, where cheeses were once stored, has been remodeled to look like an English pub.

extreme, she determined that she would build no less than a mansion modeled on the baroque style of Andalusia or Portugal, under whose spell she had fallen during her travels abroad.

Juana, a friend of some of the most powerful political figures of the day—General Justo, the president of Argentina from 1932–38, was one of them—put the project in the hands of her son-in-law, the architect Alejandro Bustillo. He had previously built her great Normandy-style summer place at Mar del Plata, an undertaking that made him famous and that led to his work on the oceanfront properties and casinos of Argentina's foremost Atlantic resort.

Arroyo Dulce is laid out around an arcaded central courtyard. Behind, wide pergolas lead to the swimming pool and tennis courts. The old house of the Cano family, a single-story building with a mirador, is used for guests. The new main house's Spanish style, which is in keeping with Argentina's colonial inheritance, is a 1920s revival and a feature of a number of other important estancias.

The design of the park, with its oaks, cedars, ashes, and old camphor trees, was begun by Benito Carrasco and continued by German landscape gardener G. Welther. Around 1930 he created a lake by damming the Arroyo Dulce, and this dam also generated hydroelectric power. Beyond the park herds grazed. Juana imported the first Charolais in the 1920s. Around 1950 her son-in-law, Ricardo Green, imported Canadian Holstein bulls, flying them in, to found a dairy herd. But the estancia's great wealth was and is its crops—wheat, soybeans, and maize—which thrive on the area's renowned black soil.

Above left: A field of young sunflowers.

*Above right: A late spring field
of ripe wheat.*

*Left: According to Sarmiento, immensity
was Argentina's curse. "The immensity is
everywhere," he wrote, "the plains, the
woods, the rivers are all immense; and the
horizon is always undefined . . . making it
difficult to tell where the land ends and the
sky begins."*

When Juana died in 1942, San Bartolo's nearly seventy square miles were divided;
her daughter, María Rosa Devoto, who was married to Ricardo Green, inherited
the main house. Other divisions followed. Silvia Green, Arroyo Dulce's present
owner, is the great-granddaughter of Bartolomé and Juana. She has maintained the
original Spanish style and at the same time, by using floral carpets and curtains, has
kept the interiors cheerful.

Carlos, the founder's grandson, and his wife, Yvonne Greene, are the owners of
San Bartolo. When they had to build a house of their own, they chose to remodel
an old cheese factory that stood on the property. The U-shaped building, with access
from a courtyard, has flat roofs and a pair of very visible brick towers that are
covered by vines. The park was designed by the famous yachtsman Martín Ezcurra,
who wisely counseled the owners not to tear down what was already there. In the
spacious cellar, where cheeses were once stored, the Green Devotos have installed a
bar and billiards table.

The two estancias are now run by their owners. When the new Land Tenancy
Act came into effect in 1969, the farmers who had been renting had to vacate. Some
took advantage of an offer to buy part of their leaseholdings; others chose compen-
sation. Work goes on to improve the yields of cereal crops, with a particular eye to
producing earlier harvests. Over the greater part of the two estancias, stock rearing
has been reduced in favor of arable farming.

La Biznaga
La Bellaca

Bishop's-weed—*la biznaga*—a modest plant with smooth stems and white flowers, gives its name to one of Argentina's most up-to-date rural establishments, located in the district of Roque Pérez, some eighty miles southwest of Buenos Aires. The land on which the estancia stands was bought in 1891 by Carlos L. Blaquier and Virginia de Alzaga de Blaquier. The original property of nearly ten square miles—presently it contains more than twice that—is in the hands of the founders' descendants.

In the last days of Rosas, the spot where the *casco* was eventually built had been a staging post midway between the towns of Lobos and Saladillo. It consisted of a single building, a tower-shaped, two-story house. Beside it was a bower under which steaks were grilled. La Biznaga's luxury was its ombus, the pampa's one tree (though in fact it is a gigantic shrub), which gave the place a cool shade.

At first the Blaquiers, whose family owned an estate some twelve miles away, made the trip to the property on horseback. The main house was erected between

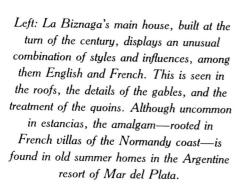

Left: La Biznaga's main house, built at the turn of the century, displays an unusual combination of styles and influences, among them English and French. This is seen in the roofs, the details of the gables, and the treatment of the quoins. Although uncommon in estancias, the amalgam—rooted in French villas of the Normandy coast—is found in old summer homes in the Argentine resort of Mar del Plata.

Right: The mansard-roofed guest house, with its recumbent lions on guard before the entrance, preceded the other buildings and was used while the main house was under construction.

103

Left: Cannas now border the old entrance to the estancia along the main road. Originally this gate was flanked by a hitching post. The pink building glimpsed among the luxuriant foliage is the estate's office.

Right: Axis deer, which come from India and Ceylon, romp in the park. The pampa's once widespread native species suffered a paradoxical reversal some seventy years ago when, in an attempt to protect the animals, estate owners kept them in semicaptivity, thereby facilitating their decimation during an epidemic of hoof-and-mouth disease. The estancia is also home to capybaras, rheas, flamingoes, and black-necked swans.

Below: Before this elaborate complex of buildings and magnificent park were created, the flat site was virtually treeless and consisted of a modest two-story house that functioned as a staging post.

Left: The oak-paneled library, with its French Empire chairs and settee, has a collection of books on art, history, and philosophy and paintings by well-known nineteenth-century artists. The still life of fruit and fish is an oil by Cándido López, famous for his epic scenes of the Paraguayan war. The smaller works are watercolors by Brazilian-born Juan León Pallière, who worked in Argentina until 1866 and left an important record of Argentine country life and customs.

Right: La Biznaga's outstanding collection of native silver includes, from top to bottom, a fiador, or horse collar; three rastras, a kind of ornamental belt buckle; and a rastra worked with gold and a series of bell stirrups from Entre Ríos.

Below: Silver and gilt matés and bombillas, *the work of River Plate craftsmen. The* bombilla *is a tube with a perforated bulb at one end that prevents the maté leaves from being sucked up. Maté was formerly drunk among all classes of Argentine society, and a rich language and tradition has grown up around it.*

1898 and 1901 and has seen successive modifications. Whether the builder was Valentín Solís or Ferruccio Togneri is unclear. Most likely each was responsible for a different stage of the work. The park, however, is the design of the renowned Carlos Thays, who laid out the tree-lined avenues and the flower beds, among which he placed Italian-style ornamentations.

In 1930 La Biznaga had some twenty model dairies. La Martona, the widely known milk producers, had installed a creamery and cheese factory at the estancia. At the time, the estate also bred shorthorn calves, which were sold off to other estancias for fattening, while better land was planted in crops by tenant farmers for a percentage of the profits. Around 1960 this system was seen to be holding back an overdue updating of the way the estate was run. To justify the investments required for such changes, the indivisibility of the land had to be guaranteed. In Argentina, where property is divided equally among all offspring, disagreements frequently result in land being sold off in sections. To prevent this, in 1961 Carlos Pedro Blaquier presented La Biznaga's heirs with an option. They could either sell their most valuable land, leaving each of them free to do what he wanted with his share of the proceeds, or they could set up a company that would assure the farm's integrity. The family chose the latter course; certain assets were sold to raise capital, and a thoroughly modern agricultural industry was created.

La Biznaga, S.A., bought two other estates, Magdala and La Bellaca, located in the districts of 25 de Mayo and Pehuajó, respectively. The company's first board of directors—which has been presided over by Carlos Herminio Blaquier since 1989—was made up of Agustina Peña de Oliveira César, Alejandro Peña Blaquier,

Juan Ignacio Blaquier, Carlos Pedro Tadeo Blaquier, Nelly Arrieta de Blaquier, Pedro C. Blaquier, Carlos M. F. Blaquier, Martín Carlos Pedro Blaquier, Rafael Alejandro de Oliveira Cezar, and Ernesto H. Pemberton.

Changes were quick to come. The ideal of cattle management is to control the complete cycle of breeding and fattening, which leaves a rancher less vulnerable to price fluctuations. To achieve this, good land is needed for fattening. This is why La Biznaga acquired the two other estates. It also did away with its own dairies, and tenant farming was replaced by large-scale agriculture, for which plowing and sowing equipment was bought and storage silos erected.

In 1961 Nelly Arrieta de Blaquier began to remodel and refurnish the house, working with the architect Emilio Maurette; with Carlos Thays III she also undertook to modernize the park. The main house is appointed with antique furniture and holds a collection of colonial silver. Among the outstanding pieces are a chiffonier, an old piano, a colonial chest of drawers, and a seventeenth-century Italian walnut refectory table. English chandeliers of crystal, opaline, and brass illuminate the rooms.

Left: La Bellaca's airy porch, with its tiled floor, iron railings and columns, and wicker furniture, is still redolent of long fin-de-siècle summers.

Right: Diana the huntress stalks the lawn in front of La Bellaca's main house. It was built in 1904, of rendered brick, and certain elements, including the ornamentation over the right-hand windows and on the parapet, suggest the influence of the Art Nouveau movement, which enjoyed great vogue in Buenos Aires. The marble statue dates from 1900.

The 2,000-acre breeding farm with its training track and stables for 214 horses.

Left: Grooms at work in the stable block. Created in 1972, the stud farm marks the Blaquier family's passion for racehorses.

Throughout the house are pictures of nineteenth-century Argentine rural life, painted by such renowned artists as Pueyrredón, Pellegrini, Rugendas, Pallière, and Blanes. There is a splendid Monvoisin, which depicts Garibaldi and his companion Anita wrapped in black-bordered red ponchos. The collection of native Argentine silver, admired by visiting princes and heads of state, includes riding crops, knives, belt buckles, bridles, spurs, stirrups, jugs, and salvers.

The park and its shallow lakes are home to abundant wildlife. There are deer, rheas (the native ostrich), and capybaras (the largest of all rodents), as well as flamingoes and black-necked swans. There are also aviaries, where golden and silver pheasants are raised together with red partridges and Colvert ducks. Peacocks stroll the lawns.

Behind the *casco* are showgrounds with wire pens and a concrete grandstand, where the establishment's cattle are sold. Among leafy trees at the far end of the park stands a strange sculpture, the work of Carlos de la Cárcova. Its great slabs of greenish bronze, divided into six panels, present the various stages of the history of La Biznaga—and of Argentina itself—from the viewpoint of the Blaquier family.

La Biznaga's racing stable is located at the estancia La Bellaca ("the knave"). This stud farm, created in 1972, is a mark of the passion for racehorses that the founder of La Biznaga handed down to his descendants. Green blouse, pink sleeves and cap are the stable's colors. It occupies nearly two thousand acres of land. Its Spanish colonial-style buildings consist of an administrative center flanked by rows of stalls. These buildings, a training track, and other open spaces are enclosed by a plantation of trees.

Santa Cándida

The province of Entre Ríos, immediately north of Buenos Aires, derives its name from the fact that it lies wedged between two of South America's great rivers, the Paraná and the Uruguay. Hence the province's common designation, the Mesopotamia of Argentina. One of the chief physical features of Entre Ríos is the vast delta along its southern reaches, which has given the province something of the character of an island. Another feature is its chains of rolling hills known as *cuchillas*, large parts of which were once heavily wooded. Other areas of the province enjoy a subtropical climate and abound in palm trees and citrus groves. As the hillier terrain is often broken or steep, thereby differing from the flat grassland of the classic pampa, the gaucho of Entre Ríos developed a riding style distinct from his Buenos Aires counterpart. Some experts claim that the *entrerriano* is the better horseman. According to the Scottish writer R. B. Cunninghame Graham, "They rolled their cigarettes and struck a light from flint and steel, all at a gallop, and on horses which, if you touched them accidentally, were almost sure to buck."

Left: In the whole of Santa Cándida the only furniture surviving from the Urquiza period (1860s) is a bed and two sofas. Here in the dining room the chairs are copies of an Empire design. The marble bust of Apollo, like all the other sculpture in the house and park, was brought from Italy by the former owners. The tapestry, an admirable complement to the statue, is modern.

Right: The ample loggia overlooks the river and is used as a kind of open-air living room. Its floor is opulently paved with marble—the black squares from Belgium, the white from Carrara. The figure is one of a pair of wild-eyed Bacchantes that flank the loggia's central archway.

Left: After the fall of Rosas in 1852, a new postcolonial architecture was introduced into Argentina; an influx of Italian architects, engineers, master builders, and stonemasons at the time assured that the predominant style would be neo-Renaissance. Built in 1858–61 by the Lombard Pedro Fossati, Santa Cándida shows clear Palladian influences in its noble proportions and its urbanity. Palladian too are its colonnaded loggia and double pilasters. Having the walls on different planes creates an exciting play of light and shade, caught perfectly here in the warm

John Lee

For over thirty years, John Lee has explored the photog̃, mastering traditional and digital photography and gra̧ profound joy and deep appreciation of both the natural images that directly convey his vision, John hopes to ill ally ethereal and at times striking compositions.

Coming of age amid the tumultuousness of Berkeley in thirties. In 1998, John began to devote himself fully to his current portfolio. John's explorations have taken hi̧ Europe. This journey can be seen in his current studies.

Much of his work could be considered hyper-realism ̧ abstract pieces are an attempt to look beneath the surfa̧ both evocative and illuminative at the same time. In ḩ space and an underlying vision of the common exposed by avid attention to detail and a devotion to creating a art as, " an exploration of the natural world, the world begin by shooting well defined photographic images. I ̧ underlying nuance and character. Finally, I reunify aņ boldly. But always attempting to look beyond the muņ.

*6065 SW Glenbrook Road • Beaverton, O̧
john@johnleeart.com •*

carcasses and salting beef and hides, for Santa Cándida is today ranked among the two or three finest examples of the architecture of its period in Entre Ríos.

The province was not an organized entity until 1822. Later in the century it was opened up to systematic immigration by land-hungry Europeans. Families of Germans, French, Swiss, Italians, Belgians, Poles, and Russian Jews arrived in droves. There were even Volga Germans. As early as 1824 the Río de la Plata Agricultural Association, of London, assisted the settling of a number of English entrepreneurs along the Uruguay River. One of their estancias, visited in the 1840s by William MacCann on his epic 2,000-mile journey on horseback through the Argentine provinces, was said to be "the largest extent of territory belonging to any British subject in this part of the world." Some 250,000 head of cattle roamed the establishment, a number too vast to be of use to their owners when there were no cowhands to keep them domesticated.

Before the age of refrigeration, such cattle were processed in *saladeros*, or beef-salting plants. The flesh, cut into half-inch-thick strips, was piled in squares of about six by six yards consisting of alternate layers of beef and salt. A day later the meat was turned over; in three days it was washed in brine and dried in the sun. In summer, three more days were sufficient for completing the process. The resulting jerked beef was barreled and shipped to Brazil and Cuba as cheap food for their slave populations. The salting factory also prepared hides and steamed the carcasses of oxen in huge vats. After twelve hours liquid tallow was drawn off into casks.

Santa Cándida, in its period of greatest splendor, was not strictly an estancia but a *saladero*. Here the eminent nineteenth-century caudillo General Justo José de Urquiza centered his operations for the export of salted meat and hides. Today the property belongs to one of the general's grandsons, Francisco José Sáenz Valiente. He and

Left: A second-floor guest room, with a glimpse into the dressing room beyond. The canopied daybed, rectangular and architecturally massive, is a characteristic Empire piece. The rocking chair is Victorian.

Above: This corridor leads onto the terrace above the loggia.

his wife, Helena Zimmerman, have opened their house to paying guests, offering them a rare opportunity to share briefly in the life of an estancia. Santa Cándida stands on the banks of the Arroyo de la China, a tributary of the Uruguay River, nearly two hundred miles north of Buenos Aires.

The main house, a building in the Italian style, is the work of architect Pedro Fossati, who also designed Urquiza's own San José Palace. Around 1850, when Santa Cándida became the first establishment of its kind in Entre Ríos, the *saladero* (also known as a *grasería*, or tallow works) consisted of a large open area, a shed for drying the jerked beef, a warehouse for salting the meat and hides, a salt store, a blacksmith's forge, soap and candle works, a carpenter's shop, and a tannery. From a navigational standpoint the establishment was strategically located for direct shipment to foreign markets, and ships of many countries called there.

This thriving trade gave life to the province and helped pay for Urquiza's costly personal expenses as well as his no less costly political ambitions, which went beyond Entre Ríos. Despite Rosas's attempt to prohibit foreign ships from plying the rivers of the Argentine interior, commerce at Santa Cándida never stopped. As soon as the process of freezing meat was invented, the beef-salting works was converted into a modern slaughterhouse. But everything disintegrated in 1870 when Urquiza was assassinated and the province was plunged into a period of instability and civil war. The general had fathered a number of illegitimate children. To cover the costs of the ensuing disputed succession, Santa Cándida was sold off. It passed into the hands of the Unzué family, who, although they owned properties throughout Argentina, made Santa Cándida their summer residence.

After Antonio Leloir and Adela Unzué de Leloir inherited Santa Cándida, they gave the estancia its present-day lines. They developed the park, incorporating Italian statuary into it, and filled the house with art objects. They also turned the establishment into one of the country's most famous breeding farms for Aberdeen Angus cattle. As a result of the economic slump of the 1930s, however, the Leloirs were forced to sell off the land bit by bit. By 1950 the property's chief income seemed to derive from the sale of gravel from the banks of the river. Finally, when the estate was reduced to little more than its *casco*, Sáenz Valiente was able to realize his dream of buying what had once been the property of his family. That was back in the early 1970s. The house was in such a sorry state that its new owner was under the impression that more rain came down inside it than out. From then on, repairs to the place became a continuous affair.

Today, as a residence, Santa Cándida is tastefully decorated and comfortable. In its black-and-white tiled drawing room are mirrors that once belonged to Sarah Bernhardt, a piece of iron grillwork from Venice, and hanging lamps in the style of Seville. From the cool of the porch in the early evening one still looks out on a river landscape that differs little from the view Cunninghame Graham saw over a century ago, when "herons and pink flamingoes sat and fished contemplatively, and on the gaunt dead branches of the willows vultures sat and nodded in the sun."

118   Entre Ríos Province

San José

The San José Palace, the main house of the estancia of the same name, was begun in 1848 and finished ten years later. By 1935 it no longer functioned as a rural establishment, and in 1937 it became a National Historical Museum dedicated to the memory of its founder, General Justo José de Urquiza (1811–70). Urquiza is a major figure in Argentine history: a wily, ruthless caudillo with the power of life and death over his gaucho followers, the general who brought an end to the rule of Rosas, a leading proponent of Argentine constitutional reform, and the first president of the Argentine Confederation.

But Urquiza's personal fortune came before his public career. He first went into business in Concepción del Uruguay with a general store. Then, buying more and more land, he came to possess seven hundred leagues—over six thousand seven hundred square miles—in Entre Ríos. From there to the provincial government was but an easy step.

Left: A string of patios, or courtyards, was a common feature of Argentine urban architecture throughout the colonial period. Unlike the first courtyard at San José, however, such patios were not arcaded on all sides. Surrounding the courtyard in the foreground here were Urquiza's private apartments, the dining room, grand drawing room, and billiards room as well as family bedrooms and state bedrooms for distinguished guests. The household staff occupied the rooms around the second courtyard.

Right: San José, begun by Italian architect Jacinto Dellepiane, was the first of Pedro Fossati's commissions for General Urquiza, the powerful Entre Ríos political chief. Urquiza's "Palace," as it was known, took ten years to build and was finished in 1858. The basic plan—towers and a single story with rooms built around a succession of courtyards—derives from Spain but is largely vernacular. Such scale and opulence, however, were unknown in Argentine rural estates of that day.

Above: A visitor to the house reported that "All the rooms are luxuriantly fitted up in the Louis Quinze style of thick curtains, heavy carpets, and massive furniture." A number of the public rooms had coffered ceilings, and that of the drawing room was inset with mirrors. This is one of the bedrooms.

Left: As president of the Argentine Confederation and governor of Entre Ríos Province, Urquiza entertained bishops, admirals, foreign ministers, and other governors. The table in this dining room is thirty feet long. The paintings between the windows are battle scenes of the Paraguayan war by Cándido López, who was so severely wounded in the battle of Curupaytí in 1866 that he had to retrain himself to paint with his left hand.

San José was meant to provide a proper setting for Urquiza's national political aspirations, a mansion befitting his greatness. The site was a secure one—about eighteen miles from Concepción del Uruguay, with the Gualeguaychú River at its back, in the heart of the loyal province of Entre Ríos. As was his style, Urquiza personally supervised the work, commissioned at the outset to Jacinto Dellepiane and at a later stage to Pedro Fossati, who had built a palace for Mehemet Ali in Egypt.

The mansion's rectangular ground plan is divided into two equal sections, each with an interior courtyard. The facade is flanked by two miradors, between which runs a gallery with seven arches supported by columns of the Tuscan order. At first, local materials were used: lime and plaster from the banks of the Paraná River; timber from the two provinces to the north, Corrientes and Misiones; and flagstone from the Uruguay River. Later, sumptuous elements were imported: Carrara marble, stone from La Spezia, tiles from the Pas de Calais, Brazilian pine, and French mirrors.

Eighteen rooms for the use of the Urquiza family and distinguished guests opened onto the first courtyard. Among these chambers were the great dining room, with its thirty-foot-long table, and the general's study and bedroom. The second courtyard, what Argentines call "the patio of the grapevine," contained a marble wellhead, a grape arbor, and a few citrus trees. Other bedrooms and dining rooms opened onto this courtyard. There were also the numerous outbuildings required of an establishment of such magnitude: coach houses, stables, dovecotes, bread ovens, a flour mill, and a general store for provisioning a staff of around 150. The kitchen was very modern, and from 1856 on the bathrooms had running water. Cunninghame Graham, visiting

Left: Made of copper latticework on an Italian marble base, this aviary is one of a pair created by Tomás Benvenuto in 1864. Each was said to have cost a thousand sovereigns. Urquiza filled these cages with canaries and with Argentine and Brazilian birds.

Top right: The chapel is a separate building behind the main house. The Italian style is everywhere apparent in this cupola designed by Fossati and decorated by the Uruguayan painter Juan Manuel Blanes.

Bottom right: The chapel's baptismal font.

the palace not long after Urquiza's death, called it "a Moorish-Spanish-looking house; inside a mixture of the house of a conquistador and a French brothel, and serving in itself as an apt illustration of the culture of the country under the general's rule."

The park was carefully looked after. Urquiza had a taste for rare plant species, and on his travels to Asunción and Buenos Aires he was forever bringing back attractive specimens. A garden in front of the house, surrounded by an iron fence, offered one kind of habitat, but the grounds also contained exotic nooks with tropical birds in copper latticework aviaries set on marble bases, and coconut palms, cork oaks, araucarias, and banana trees. Some of these trees had been the gift of don Pedro II, Emperor of Brazil. In 1854 the estancia tried out crops like peanuts, cassava, and tea, as well as plots of wheat and maize. There was also an orchard with a wide variety of fruit trees.

In 1853 San José had about seventy thousand sheep, forty thousand cattle, and two thousand horses. Nearby, a farming community was established, its immigrants hailing from Switzerland, France, Germany, Piedmont, and Savoy. Unlike many of the great landowners of the day, Urquiza saw quite early that the country's agricultural future did not lie only in cattle.

San José 123

Left: The rooms enclosing San José's second patio included the kitchen, a private secretary's office, and quarters for aides-de-camp, governess, housemaids, and cook. The wellhead was carved from a single piece of marble and stands over a cistern that originally collected rainwater. Orange or lemon trees were common in such courtyards; here the grapevine, growing on an ironwork trellis, provides welcome shade in summer.

Right: The rear gate, with the chapel on the right. The palace's grounds were extensive and included groves of peach, quince, pear, pomegranate, apple, and fig trees. General Urquiza's assassins entered the house throught this gate in 1870.

The caudillo spent the best part of the last twenty-two years of his life in the chambers and gardens of the palace. As president of the Argentine Confederation in the years 1854–60, he went to Paraná, the provisional capital, no more than was necessary. Instead, he remained at San José, where, besides occupying his time with politics and diplomacy, he presided over litigation among his neighbors and managed his numerous farming and industrial interests. At the same time, a complicated family life kept him busy, for the general had had many lovers and a large number of illegitimate children, whom he legitimized by an act of Congress. Dolores Costa, his companion and wife during his final years, was mistress of San José.

Urquiza relived one of his hours of triumph on 3 February 1870, the eighteenth anniversary of the battle of Caseros, in which he had defeated Rosas. His former adversary, the new president of Argentina, Domingo F. Sarmiento, paid him an official visit. For the occasion, the main courtyard was converted into a dance floor and the artificial lake near the house became the scene of a Venetian aquatic festival. One witness claimed the celebration had been worthy of the court of Louis XIV; another compared it to the tournaments of medieval castles. Two months later, however, on 11 April, the caudillo's refuge became a deadly trap. On that day a party in the pay of his rival Ricardo López Jordán broke into San José's rear gate to cries of "Death to the traitor Urquiza!" The general tried vainly to defend himself. He fell in his bedroom, mortally wounded by a shot in the face, and was repeatedly stabbed. He died in the arms of his wife and daughters, who had witnessed the scene. The bloodstained traces of this tragedy can still be seen on the room's walls.

San Pedro

San Pedro, one of the oldest and most famous estancias in Entre Ríos, once comprised 270 square miles of land in the rolling country of the province's long central chain of hills, the Cuchilla Grande, which parallels the Uruguay River.

In 1791 Villa del Arroyo de la China (the present-day town of Concepción del Uruguay) granted Pedro Prellezzó, a Spaniard, the right to set up an estancia on land running from the bank of the Gualeguaychú River nine or ten miles west to the bank of the Gená. Prellezzó was to become one of the richest cattlemen of the region. He built his house on the Arroyo de los Pájaros, and eventually both stream and establishment came to be known as the Rincón de San Pedro, after the saint's day of the property's first owner.

The name Gená is a reference to the small, warlike tribe of Charrúa Indians, who were the area's original inhabitants. Fierce defenders of their freedom, they withstood submission to the Spaniards and even rejected the preaching of the Jesuits. These aboriginals were exterminated sometime in the seventeenth century. Their territory

Left: Like so much else in this part of Entre Ríos, San Pedro once belonged to General Urquiza. From the air the present-day casco, set in its 500-acre park, has the appearance of a tidy suburban village.

Right: The large, comfortable house was built in 1928 in the style that Argentines call a chalet. The chimneys and half-timber construction suggest an English Tudor influence, while the roof treatment and general roominess are reminiscent of Edwardian country houses. Incorporated in the heart of the structure are the four rooms built in 1872 by Urquiza's daughter.

Left: Newly planted rice fields under the immense Argentine sky.

Right: A modern galvanized-iron shed is the twentieth-century ranch hand's matera. *Here a group sits smoking and brewing maté. The man on the right, for some reason wearing the kind of hat used by his counterpart in southern Brazil, pours hot but not boiling water from a kettle (called the* pava *or* caldera) *into his maté, which is half filled with crushed yerba leaves. The leaves swell, more water is added, the bombilla is carefully inserted, and the resulting infusion is then shared. The cup is continually refilled with hot water and passed around until the leaves lose their flavor.*

Below: Peones *training a troop of horses. The palisaded corral is still common in wooded areas and harks back to a time before the introduction of wire fencing.*

Left: The house has two entrance halls.
This one, turned into a sitting room, has an
eclectic mix of unpretentious furnishings.
Beamed ceilings of various styles are a
feature of many of the rooms.

Right: This bedroom, with its dark wood
colonial furniture (including a prie-dieu),
silver toilet set, crystal candlesticks, gaslit
chandelier, and religious pictures, evokes
perfectly the atmosphere of a bygone era.

came to be occupied by no more than a dozen white settlers who made a living by cutting wood, which they fashioned into posts or made into charcoal, and by trading in hides, ostrich products, horses, and cattle.

The estancia was sold to Pantaleón Panelo in 1816 and acquired thirty years later by General Urquiza. In 1860 twenty square miles were added to the forty it contained at the time. During the war of the Triple Alliance—fought from 1865–70 between Paraguay, on one side, and Argentina, Uruguay, and Brazil on the other—the establishment was a depot for supplying cattle and horses to the Allied armies. At one point the number of mounts was so vast that on breaking out of their corral they stampeded and killed several of their drovers.

On 11 April 1870 a party headed by Nico Coronel, San Pedro's foreman, secretly left the estancia and made its way to San José, some eighteen miles distant, where they stormed Urquiza's palace. Were their orders to take the general prisoner and force him to resign his post as governor or were they simply to kill him? When Urquiza tried to defend himself, Coronel dispatched him with his knife.

Once the national government had put down the Entre Ríos uprising, the complicated succession to the caudillo's property could be dealt with. San Pedro passed on to one of Urquiza's daughters, Justa, who at the age of eighteen had married an army officer, Luis María Campos. On three different occasions he served as Argentina's minister of war. The Campos family pulled down the big old house where Urquiza's assassin had lived, and in 1872 they built the four rooms that became the heart of the new residence. They also carried out a series of agricultural improvements that were perhaps the most advanced in the province up until that time.

The land was divided into sections and fenced; the damming of streams was replaced by windmill pumps; and, thanks to the efforts of Russian-German settlers from the Volga, 115 square miles were brought under cultivation. To improve the livestock, the estancia was turned into an experimental center for combatting insect pests, such as ticks, and diseases like sheep scab. The province's first dipping vats were installed at San Pedro.

By 1933, when General Campos had died and his son, Adolfo, was running the estancia, the bread ovens, carpenter's shop, and smithy had been modernized, and refrigeration and electricity-generating plants were installed. There were also an aviary and facilities for poultry and pheasant breeding. The estancia's owners now went directly to the port of Buenos Aires to hire newly arrived immigrants, whom they then trained. As the majority of the farmhands were local people, however, the estancia always preserved its old Argentine character.

Owing to the solidarity of the Campos Urquiza children—Jorge, Justita, Haydée, and María Cristina—the estancia survived the economic plight of the 1930s. The last named had married Horacio Bustos Morón. The only offspring of their marriage, María Cristina, died in 1986. She had been the wife of Carlos Alberto Roca, the lawyer who administered the family properties in the 1950s, a time when direct management took over from tenant farming, the premises were electrified, and more successful crops, such as rice, were introduced. The trend today has been toward conservation, with aerial sowing and reduced tillage. María Cristina Campos Urquiza de Bustos Morón, the owner of San Pedro, handed the running of the estancia over to her grandsons, Jorge and Carlos Roca Bustos.

The park of almost five hundred acres, adorned with electrically illuminated lampposts and gates from France, provides a proper setting for the main house, which, with its mock-Tudor and baronial elements, was built in 1928 by the architectural firm of Sánchez, Lagos, and de la Torre. San Pedro boasts a collection of Spanish ceramics, colonial silver, English furniture, and objects like the pair of inkwells presented by the Paraguayan dictator Francisco Solano López to Urquiza in memory of the former's services as mediator in 1859, when the pact of San José de Flores—which provided for the incorporation of Buenos Aires Province into the Argentine Confederation—was signed.

The memory of the Entre Ríos caudillo is everywhere—in the gardens, where a monument evokes those who fell in the battle of Caseros, when his troops defeated Rosas, and even on the walls of the house, where Urquiza looks down on the visitor in two celebrated portraits, one by Baldassare Verazzi and the other by the Uruguayan master Juan Manuel Blanes, who made the Entre Ríos chieftain pose for posterity in civilian dress.

Santa Catalina

The province of Córdoba, whose capital lies four hundred miles northwest of Buenos Aires midway to the Andes, straddles a line that divides the humid pampa, to the east and south, from the dry pampa, to the north and west. In the subregion of the high pampa, where the plains end and the foothills of the sierra begin, the slopes are clothed in scrubby, thorny trees and shrubs, including native species like the *espinillo*, *chañar*, *algarrobo*, and *tala*. Here, in 1573, conquistadors going south on the trade route from the mining region of present-day Bolivia to the River Plate founded the city of Córdoba, the site of Argentina's oldest university.

Early in the seventeenth century the Jesuits arrived in Córdoba and began buying land with the aim of building estancias to support their religious and educational work. A number of these former properties of the Society of Jesus are still extant, and one—Santa Catalina—is among the most harmonious and best preserved monuments of colonial architecture in the whole province. The Jesuits paid forty-five

Left: One of the cloister's vaulted passageways. After Córdoba's first kiln was built in 1601, brick and tile replaced mud walls and straw roofs. Santa Catalina is among the best preserved of the Jesuit estancias of the province.

Right: The Jesuits arrived in Córdoba in 1599 and, among other activities, developed huge estancias. Counting many exceptional architects among them, they made the province the outstanding center of colonial architecture in Argentina. Santa Catalina's church and monastery, begun around 1750 and built in the baroque style, was part of a large estancia complex.

hundred pesos, a considerable sum at the time, for land forty-five miles north of the city of Córdoba at what is today Ascochinga but was then Indian territory that had been granted to conquistador Miguel de Ardiles. On the estate, cattle, sheep, and mules were bred, and, by the use of artificial irrigation, the soil was cultivated. To bring water from the distant mountains of Ongamira, a stone aqueduct was built. The flow provided power for two of the estancia's mills as well; the establishment also functioned as a small center for cottage industries, producing cloth, which was woven and dyed, and soap. A large slave population—more than four hundred native- and African-born blacks—worked at these tasks, together with the remnants of subjugated Indian tribes.

Construction of Santa Catalina's church was begun around 1750. The design, with nave, transept, and dome, has been attributed to Fray Antonio Harls, who was born in Bavaria in 1725. The graceful bell towers and baroque facade are reminiscent of the churches of southern Germany and Austria. Set back and to one side of the church proper is the cloister. Tradition says that the Jesuit historians Father Lozano and Father Guevara lived in the high-ceilinged rooms and that a famous Italian musician, Domenico Zipoli, died here and is buried in the church's small cemetery. The cemetery is approached through a gate of exceptional beauty, tinged with a greenish patina. Other buildings include a novitiate, storerooms, and workshops. There is even an underground passage for escaping in the event of a siege.

The cloister was unfinished when the Jesuits were expelled from Spain and the Spanish Crown's New World territories in 1767. For a number of years Santa Catalina's artistic wealth was subject to pillage and destruction. Then, in 1774, the

The church's gilded wood altarpiece, with its polychromed figures, also contains a painting of the establishment's patron saint. Such details as the sharply projecting entablatures and the beveled plane between the pilasters (where a censer hangs on the right) are hallmarks of baroque architectural style.

board of temporalities, which was in charge of administering the Jesuits' sequestered properties and effects, sold the establishment to the mayor of the city of Córdoba. Francisco José Díaz paid ninety-nine thousand pesos for the estancia; he undertook to keep the church in good repair and to maintain a chaplain. He also finished work on the cloister. From that time on, descendants of the Córdoba mayor have been the estancia's owners.

So it was that Santa Catalina entered a new stage at the center of the province's political life. "From my country estate I have been called to this city to take up the powers that an election has conferred on me," declared Colonel José Javier Díaz (1764–1829), the mayor's son and heir to his substantial fortune and political career. In 1815 this rancher-soldier proclaimed the autonomy of the province and its opposition to the centralism of Buenos Aires. His biographers say that on the two occasions he served as governor he maintained a calm, careful style in a period of violent passions. A jealous partisan of authority—he reestablished flogging as a punishment for many crimes—Díaz became an efficient instrument of the province's ruling class, by which it adapted to the new times with a minimum of change.

The bitter civil war of the 1830s and 1840s did not spare the estancia. General Manuel Oribe, who led Rosas's army against the Unitarians in the north of Argentina, made Santa Catalina his headquarters. One of José Javier's daughters, Guillermina Díaz de Frías, an intelligent, beautiful woman, pleaded with Oribe not to confiscate the estate. "The request of so brave and fair a lady is worthy of my word," the general gallantly assured her. So the Díaz family did not suffer forfeiture, the penalty paid in that day by a political enemy. On another occasion, when a Federal raiding party sacked the estancia, Felipe Díaz made a miraculous escape and promised that every year thereafter, on the last Sunday of January, a mass and procession would be held at Santa Catalina in commemoration of the event.

This tradition is kept up by the present owners of the estate, members of the de la Torre, Díaz, Gavier, and Martínez families, some 150 of whom have the right to inhabit the establishment's "rooms." Each of these quarters has its own dining room and kitchen. The owners are responsible for preserving the character of what is today a national monument and allowing public access to it.

Successions and the selling off of land have reduced the property's former 230 square miles to its present 2,000 acres. Nowadays native cattle are raised and maize is grown on leased farms. The church regains its old splendor on ceremonial occasions, when dressed-up images of saints are taken outdoors. Santa Catalina is paraded about on the shoulders of the men of the house; San José, by descendants of the one-time servants. After a turn around the water reservoir, the saints are returned to the church, and friends and family, who have come expressly to take part in the festivities, enjoy a sumptuous repast.

San Nicolás

The province of Santa Fe, immediately north of Buenos Aires and bordered on the east for hundreds of miles by the mighty Paraná River, was of importance in colonial days for its strategic location along the commercial lifeline both upriver to Asunción and overland to the interior and the north. But it was not until late in the last century that the province's true potential as rich agricultural land could be exploited. Until then there simply were not people enough to make farming viable. When Darwin set out on his three-hundred-mile journey from Buenos Aires to the city of Santa Fe in 1833 he saw along the way ransacked, deserted houses, and his chief fear was of being waylaid by Indians. Fifteen years later another English traveler, William MacCann, noted that a certain sixty-thousand-acre estancia he visited ("one of the finest in the province") was unstocked and that although its soil was extremely fertile and "every inch ready for the plough" only a bit of flax was growing there. By the 1920s, however, the port of Rosario, which had been a sleepy town of four thousand inhabitants when MacCann set foot in it, was Argentina's Chicago—its

Left: As early as 1845, Sarmiento pointed out that Argentine boys learned to ride as soon as they learned to walk. "When they become stronger, they race over the country, falling off their horses and getting up again, tumbling on purpose . . . and practicing feats of horsemanship." Small wonder, then, that Argentine polo players are among the finest in the world. The British introduced the game to Argentina in 1874, and the first polo club was founded in Buenos Aires eight years later. Here members of the Uranga family are at play.

Right: The facade of San Nicolás typifies the Argentine estancia of the middle of the last century. It has all the aspects of a defensive outpost, which it was; yet at the same time it has a charm and homey elegance unmatched by the extravagant creations built in better times some fifty years later by many Argentine cattlemen.

second city—with a large population and vast exports of wheat and beef. Santa Fe had become the nation's breadbasket.

The story of San Nicolás begins in 1857, when Ignacio Uranga and his wife, Nicolasa Montaner, bought nearly two hundred square miles of land south of Rosario. The property was crossed by a rivulet, the Pavón, a natural watering place without which any attempt to raise cattle would have been unfeasible. At the time, the provincial government was actively selling off public land in order to stimulate the territory's productivity, for in the aftermath of the declaration of independence from Spain in 1816 Santa Fe had become little more than a battlefield in the internecine struggles among the provinces, especially between Buenos Aires and the interior. The Cepeda and Pavón, two Santa Fe streams, are also sites of battles fought in 1820, the names of which are known to every Argentine. The result of these long years of chaos had been impoverishment.

It was not until around 1860 that great estancias began to prosper on the Santa Fe pampa. In the north, small farming communities grew up, while the south of the province supported sheep ranchers, almost all of them from Buenos Aires. Only after the 1870s did these estancias cease to need protection from the Indians. The architecture of San Nicolás bears features dating from the unsettled period of its founding: walls half a yard thick, a mirador, wrought-iron grills on all the windows, axe-hewn hardwood doors. Above the hearth hang the firearms with which the family defended itself against both Indian raider and common thief. An old stocks serves as a reminder that in those days the civil government in such out-of-the-way places ceded to a landowner's authority.

In the 1880s cattle replaced sheep, and a well was dug at the far end of the property for watering the stock. Land as rich as that of San Nicolás could maintain on each league (or 6,000 acres) between 2,000 and 3,000 head of cattle, 400 to 500 horses, or 4,000 to 5,000 sheep. In 1912 Italian immigrants were brought in as tenant farmers. They tilled the soil with horses, each family working about 100 acres. The estancia supported 150 families, who built themselves makeshift huts. Today the establishment's farmers live in the nearby town of Uranga.

The estancia was modernized in 1952. The founder's grandchildren and great-grandchildren formed a company, the Sociedad La Ensenada, which bought machinery, replaced the horses with 14 tractors, and renewed the livestock. Ten years later the establishment branched into seed production, for which silos and a sorting and processing shed were built. Marcos and Ignacio Uranga, the fifth generation of the family, took over and chose to run the estate themselves. The property was divided into 60 sections, and a storage facility for cereal crops, with a capacity of 9,000 metric tons, was erected in Uranga. In 1982 genetic selection and hybridization of maize, sorghum, and sunflowers was introduced. A new processing plant that packs over 50,000 pounds of seed a day was built in 1984.

Personnel to fill the estancia's increasingly technical positions is often recruited from professionally qualified family members, who gather for meetings at the estancia twice a year. There they also enjoy their favorite sport—polo.

Right: The restraint of the structural and decorative elements in this passageway— salmon-pink walls, plain wooden doors, a wicker chair, an old Indian spear, a few gigantic leaves, and plumes of pampas grass—speak of the Spartan life of the old-time estancia.

Above: Pampas grass (Cortaderia selloana) grows six to nine feet tall. Its silky, silvery flowering plumes, turned golden here in the afternoon's dying light, are a familiar sight in suburban gardens throughout the world.

Los Alamos

In the semiarid desert country of western Argentina, along the border with Chile, is the province of Mendoza. Well-watered by the rivers of the Andean cordillera, and thanks to a system of irrigation channels, parts of the region have been turned into oases that today support vineyards, olive orchards, and fruit groves. The city of Mendoza, the provincial capital, founded in 1561, boasts the third largest winery in the world.

The estate of the Bombal family, near San Rafael, 150 miles south of Mendoza and over 600 from Buenos Aires, stands in one such desert oasis. It was founded in 1820 by Juan Bombal Valenzuela, grandson of a French immigrant from Limoges, and from its earliest days cattle were raised here. Fattened on alfalfa, the herds were then driven over the 9,000-foot Planchón Pass for sale to Chilean markets. Along the way the animals grazed in the high meadows of the Andes. The drovers sheltered in stone huts without roofs (the heavy snows would have collapsed them), which they

Left: Built in 1830, Los Alamos is said to be the oldest house to survive the earthquake that devasted Mendoza Province in 1861. Here a courtyard is screened by a forged iron gate. The simple architectural style is a throwback to southern Spain of an earlier period.

Right: A set of bentwood tables and chairs, a design mass-produced in Vienna by Michael Thonet in the latter half of the nineteenth century, matches the informality and simplicity of the terrace.

Right: Mature vines thrust their roots deeply into the soil. Argentina is the fifth largest wine-producing country in the world and ranks fourth in per capita consumption.

Above: The estate takes its name from the poplars that divide the vineyard's herringbone-patterned layout. The New World's first vines were brought by Spanish missionaries to Mexico in 1520. Mendoza's vineyards are 3,500 feet above sea level and account for seventy percent of Argentina's wine production.

Left: Here in the cellars of Los Alamos, as elsewhere, full-bodied red wines are left to age in oak casks. The staves, which are porous, allow oxygen through to the wine and give it a distinctive flavor.

covered over with the branches of shrubs. In those days, crops were of no economic interest in that part of Mendoza and would not be for some time. In 1880 San Rafael's military garrison still protected the southern frontier from Indian attacks.

The lucrative cattle trade was interrupted by the war of independence, which generated a new style of banditry. Its leading figures were two Chilean brothers by the name of Pincheyra. Because they headed up a band of Araucanian Indians, one became known as the *cacique blanco*, the "white chief." For years—or so it was said—the Pincheyras were masters of the southern part of the province and kept stolen cattle in stone corrals near the border in Malargüe before selling them across the frontier.

Meanwhile, one of Juan's sons, Domingo Bombal Ugarte, was on several occasions a member of the interim government of Mendoza. He signed the decree by which the city was relocated after an earthquake destroyed the capital in 1861. His wife, Nemesia Videla, and their three daughters lost their lives in the destruction. Despite the disaster, he went on buying land and in 1866 he acquired nearly forty square miles suitable for irrigation near San Rafael. Although he seldom visited his properties, he nonetheless organized a system of four staging posts to connect the province's capital to its southern reaches, a region whose land began to increase in value.

Domingo's younger son, Domingo Bombal Videla, who never got over his mother's death, went to live in San Rafael, where he extended the family's property. According to a survey of the period, it reached all the way to the Chilean border in the high cordillera. In addition to Los Alamos, his other estates included El Nevado and Laguna Blanca, the site of Las Leñas, Argentina's most sophisticated resort for

This corner of the conservatory, used for card playing, serving drinks, and as a reading room, is brightened by a varied collection of brass objects, including the brazier mounted high up on the wall. The chest under the samovar is an old Spanish piece. The ironwork grill over the window is a reminder of the protection from Indian marauders that the estate required until the 1880s.

winter sport. Bombal Videla took part in driving the cattle raised on his estancia to market in Chile. Possibly inspired by his French forebear, he also planted magnificent vineyards, with choice grapes, on acreage bordered by rows of the poplars that gave the estate its name.

In that day, wine-making was a pioneer enterprise. The slow transport by mule team on the long journey to Buenos Aires spoiled the wine before it reached its principal market of consumption. For this reason, as his father before him had been instrumental in bringing the stagecoach to San Rafael, Domingo fought to bring the railroad to the area. The last track was laid in 1908, just after he had died in the dining room of Los Alamos.

His widow, Susana Hughes, failed to take advantage of the economic expansion brought by the railroad. Having no interest in Los Alamos, she rented the property out and went to live in Buenos Aires, where she attended to the education of her three daughters. At the age of twenty-eight and just married, one of them—Susana Bombal Hughes—decided to return to her childhood home. Twenty years had passed; she found all the original furniture gone, and the ditch that surrounded the *casco* had turned into a mire. Undeterred, Susana began the restoration of Los Alamos, ultimately imbuing it with her unique touch.

From her European trips she brought back furniture, fabrics, and wallpapers. English armchairs, beds from Nice, a sculpted Virgin from Seville—things piled up until she found the right place for them. Through friendships with artists like Raúl Soldi, Héctor Basaldúa, and Norah Borges, Susana also added paintings to the house. Among the literary figures who celebrated her hospitality were Jorge Luis Borges, Manuel Mujica Láinez, and Richard Llewellyn. In a poem dating from 1970, Borges wrote that he found her singular spirit in music and

> *in the gentle*
> *blue of the sky, in Greek hexameters,*
> *in our own solitude, which seeks her out,*
> *in a fountain's mirrored waters . . .*

The estate is currently owned by Rosa Yolanda Bombal, Susana's sister, and César and Camilo Aldo Bombal, the third sister's sons. Los Alamos is the last of the original properties still in the family's hands, and they run it themselves. When ash rained down from the Chilean volcano Descabezado in 1930, causing the wholesale destruction of cattle on the ranches of southern Mendoza and San Luis provinces, agriculture took a great leap forward. The grape varieties now current at Los Alamos are French: the whites, Pinot Blanc and Chenin; and the reds, Pinot Noir, Cabernet Sauvignon, and Malbec. A Spanish variety, Pedro Ximénez, from Jerez de la Frontera, has been added to them. Of the estate's 10,000 acres, only 750 are given over to irrigated crops. Almost a third of this land is in vineyards; an equal portion is in crops such as garlic, tomatoes, and sweet peppers; and the balance is in fruit orchards, part for fresh consumption and part for canning. In one of Argentina's economic crises a few years ago, the estate's canning factory closed. The rest of the property is used for grazing cattle, such as the zebu, which is suitable for a dry climate.

Pampa Grande

The province of Salta, in the far northwest of Argentina on the frontiers with Chile and Bolivia, is a world apart from the vast flat plains bordering the Paraná and the River Plate 800 miles to the southeast. Set in a varied Andean landscape of salt basins, towering mountains (several of the region's peaks rise to over 6,000 meters, or nearly 20,000 feet), and fertile high valleys, Salta also has old colonial traditions and an ancient indigenous culture.

In one of these valleys, about a mile above sea level, is Pampa Grande, the estancia (or *finca*, as such estates are more commonly known in Salta) that has been in the Gómez Alzaga family for the last 140 years. Located in the department of Guachipas, midway between the city of Salta and the border of Tucumán, the neighboring province to the south, Pampa Grande's 115 square miles are given over almost entirely to grazing for a variety of cattle—native, brown Swiss, and zebu— as well as for Peruvian-Argentine horses, a good breed for use in mountainous terrain.

Before the Spaniards arrived in the middle of the sixteenth century, this land had been inhabited by aborigines known as the Diaguitas, or Calchaquians. (The former

Left: Cheeses made at Pampa Grande from the milk of its different cows. The red peppers, now widely cultivated in Salta Province, are also the finca's own produce.

Right: The big, old-fashioned stove in this spacious, down-to-earth kitchen is fueled by wood. The northwest region of Argentina boasts a number of traditional dishes, among them frangollo *and* chilcán, *whose principal ingredient is maize.*

was the name of their language, the latter a geographical designation.) Living in densely populated villages in buildings made of stones piled one on the other without mortar, they tilled the soil, made pottery, constructed canals to irrigate their fields of maize, potatoes, and gourds, husbanded flocks of llamas, and hunted guanacos and ostriches. They also made *chicha*, a kind of beer fermented from maize, or a similar alcoholic drink, *aloja*, made from the fruit of such native trees as the *algarrobo* and *chañar*. The Calchaquí people left images of themselves in cave paintings, in which they are decked out in tunics and feathered headdresses. Some of the best known vestiges of this valley culture are large urns, with cylindrical necks, in which the bodies of children were buried. Those that archeologists have dug up at Pampa Grande are painted with both human and animal motifs. Some of the imagery on these vessels has a dramatic realism, depicting well-crafted faces from whose slanted eyes tears fall.

The capacity and disposition to work of the Guachipas, the tribe living in the area where Pampa Grande now stands, was soon utilized by the Spanish conquerors. Governor Hernando de Lerma founded the city of Salta in 1582. He also appropriated the Guachipas as an encomienda to himself. This was a system of vassalage that exacted a tribute in labor or domestic service from the Indians "for the term of their lives and the life of one heir." Lerma, however, was unable to reap the benefits. Accused of having committed a number of wrongs while he was governor—in particular of having tortured to death his predecessor, Gonzalo de Abreu—he was tried in Spain and sentenced to death. Colonial history in northwest Argentina is a chronicle of violent deeds, including a long series of bloody uprisings by the Indians of the Calchaquí Valleys through much of the seventeenth century.

In 1622 Lerma's grandson, Bernardo de la Fresnada, is known to have laid claim to Pampa Grande for the purpose of selling it to Pedro de Abreu, the grandson of Lerma's old enemy. As the valley's new owner, Abreu renamed the property San Pedro de Buenavista. In the next century the *finca* passed into the hands of Félix de Arias Rengel, a soldier who had fought the Indians in the eastern part of the province. Owner of one of the most opulent houses in the city of Salta, he came to possess nearly the whole of the present department of Guachipas. In addition to Pampa Grande, which he bought in 1736, he acquired four other estancias.

In 1816 the *finca* changed hands again. Its new owner was General Juan Antonio Alvarez de Arenales, a Spaniard who had joined the cause of independence, rallying his laborers and fighting with generals Manuel Belgrano and José de San Martín against the Spanish Crown. Later Alvarez became provincial governor. Married to a Salta woman, he spent his last years tending his properties. It was then that the *finca*'s large homestead was built at Rincón, in the extreme south of the valley, as were its *pircas*, dry-masonry corrals made of stone torn from the ruins of the pre-Hispanic villages. The *sala*, as the owner's residence is known locally, is in the unostentatious Spanish style. Its yard-thick adobe walls are frequently painted to keep their appearance fresh. The establishment's money was made in those days by breeding mules for sale to the army or to the mines in Chile, Bolivia, and Peru.

Left: Cowhands rope cattle in a big corral, whose dry-stone construction is of Quechua origin. Such walls are known by their Quechua name—pircas.

Right: The sala, *as an estate's residence is known in Salta, nestles in a woodland thick with native species. Over sixty percent of the province is forested.*

In the 1850s Indalecio Gómez, a native of Salta, bought Pampa Grande from General Arenales's daughters. Gómez's grandson, a lawyer also called Indalecio Gómez, gave the estancia the look it has today. He was an outstanding public figure who, as secretary of the interior under President Roque Sáenz Peña, drafted the far-reaching 1912 electoral reform law that gave all Argentine males the vote by secret and compulsory ballot.

Gómez improved the house, dammed the valley's river so that summer rainfall could be used for crop irrigation, and bought two neighboring estates, increasing the establishment, which he bequeathed to his sons, Carlos and Jaime, to ninety-two square miles. The former, who married an Alzaga—a great Buenos Aires ranching family—eventually acquired the part of the estancia that had belonged to his brother. With the purchase of another two properties in 1937, the establishment he handed down to his sons, the present owners, reached its present size.

Life at Pampa Grande has changed little in the last century. As in the past, today's cowherds use *guardamontes,* a type of outsize chaps attached to the saddle rather than worn as leggings, for protection against the thorny scrub. Skilled leather-workers, these men live in isolated huts in the hills, together with their families, goats, palisaded corrals, and small plots of maize, which they cultivate in the same painstaking way as did their forebears.

El Bordo de las Lanzas

Set in the flat, fertile Siancas valley, thirty-seven miles east of the city of Salta and over twenty-five hundred feet above sea level, El Bordo de las Lanzas is one of the most historic *fincas* of the province. Its subtropical climate supports a lush vegetation, and its woods are full of pink-, yellow-, and violet-colored native trees that never lose their leaves: *lapachos*, jacarandas, *chañares, algarrobos, tipas, palos borrachos, mistoles*, and *guayacanes*. Coots, spoonbills, black-crowned night herons (known in Argentina as water foxes), and chachalacas frequent the *finca's* shallow lakes and waterways. In some of the waterways, alligators sun themselves under the protection of Las Lanzas' owners, who feel that efforts must be made to keep these reptiles reproducing.

The twenty-two hundred acres of the estate that are irrigated by the waters of the Mojotoro River produce good yields of maize, beans, tobacco, sugar cane, cotton, avocadoes, greens, cherimoyas, guavas, papayas, and other crops, many of them originally introduced from Peru. Irrigation rights for the river's waters stem from colonial times. In fact, the establishment's colonial roots go back to Juan Vázquez de Tapia, who owned the *finca* around 1609.

Left: As is fitting for a house with a fine historical pedigree, El Bordo de las Lanzas has an outstanding collection of colonial furniture. Here in the living room bright modern sofas mix well with older pieces, such as the cane-seated armchairs of French derivation and the low table. Under the stairs is a vargueño, *a writing cabinet with a drop lid, which rests on a trestle stand. The hanging carpet and the small tapestries draped over the railing are modern designs woven locally by traditional techniques.*

Right: The thick doors and heavy lintels here in another nook of the living room—and throughout the house—are original and came from timber that grew on the finca. *On the mantelpiece is displayed a pair of mud nests of the* hornero, *or ovenbird, a familiar Argentine species named for the shape of its dwelling.*

The name El Bordo de las Lanzas is made up of two parts. El Bordo is the present name of a village that once formed part of the estate and that keeps popping up and then disappearing in old documents, so that currently it is linked to this *finca* as well as to others nearby. A *lanza* is the hardwood pole, or tongue, of a heavy wagon, such as those used to haul goods to market.

The *finca* has changed owners several times in its four-hundred-year existence. In the eighteenth century it belonged to Juan Adrián Fernández Cornejo, who appeared in Salta around the time of the expulsion of the Jesuits in the 1760s and later set up the San Isidro sugar refinery, one of the oldest mills of its kind in Argentina, in the village of Campo Santo. The property, then called San Lorenzo de las Lanzas, eventually belonged to his daughter and after that to his granddaughter, Gabriela Goyechea Cornejo de Figueroa Toledo. She sold the estate to Magdalena Goyechea de Güemes, the mother of Salta's most famous patriot, Martín Miguel de Güemes, who led his unorthodox gaucho cavalry to celebrated victories over the Spaniards in the war of independence.

It was at this and other *fincas* of the department now bearing his name that General Güemes trained and transformed his militia. Argentine historian and statesman Bartolomé Mitre, in chronicling the period, wrote that Güemes taught the gauchos primitive tactics suited to their character and imagination. He "promoted their warlike instincts, stimulated individual spontaneity, and created a new spirit, which they identified with the defense of their territory and with the supreme authority of their chieftain." In their military exercises Güemes's followers "made menaces of disordered charges like Cossacks, discharged volleys into the air like Arabs, or jumped to the ground . . . now forming groups of infantry, now dispersing as sharpshooters, now mounting quickly on horseback, now concentrating rapidly with savage alacrity like the Indians of the pampas." In the field, Güemes and his gauchos were invincible and at a moment crucial to the outcome of the war they stopped the advance of the Spanish army in Upper Peru, thus ending the threat of an invasion of Argentine soil.

Meanwhile, doña Magdalena remained firmly at the helm of the family. Said to have been the prototype of the upper-class Salta woman, she was tall and imperious, the mother of a flock of offspring, with a vast troop of servants to order about. Related to everyone in local society, she was enterprising and skilled in managing her estate. She had the *finca*'s dwelling built and advanced the sugar industry, which was the region's economic mainstay.

In 1846 the establishment was sold to Miguel Antonio Figueroa. His son, José, who had made a fortune selling mules to Peru, set up a modern sugar mill with machinery imported from Liverpool. His workers were Indians from the sultry Chaco country in the eastern part of the province. Around the turn of the century, the estate came into the hands of an Algerian-born Frenchman, Olivier de Maglaive, who volunteered to return to France for service in World War I. He did little, however, to look after the *finca*. When Dario Arias Cornejo bought it in 1958, he found the *sala* in a dilapidated state. Eager to reestablish old traditions and at the same time to set up a model establishment, he unified this *finca* and two adjoining properties belonging to him under the name El Bordo de las Lanzas and began to rebuild the house. He has lived there with his wife, Graciela Iturrieta, and their children since 1973.

Architects Javier Cruz and Ana Iturrieta de Cruz and engineer Guillermo Solá Figueroa were commissioned to carry out the restoration. The *sala*'s basic structure and colonial character were preserved, but adaptations were made so as to include

Luxuriant foliage and red blossoms, contrasting with the clean lines and stark white walls of the sala, *are the courtyard's chief adornment.*

modern comforts. The house is built mainly of adobe brick and hardwoods—*arca*, *algarrobo*, and cinchona—from the *finca*'s own forest. The building's thick walls had managed to withstand a number of earthquakes through the years, so the original heavy lintels and doors, with their old iron locks, were still intact. Other elements, however, had to be bought from demolition sites. Luckily, the bricks, roof tiles, floor tiles, doors, windows, and beams of colonial structures were made to standard measures.

The *sala* built by Güemes's mother at the end of the eighteenth century, with its classical layout—central courtyard surrounded by verandas onto which the rooms open—is now the setting for an important collection of colonial furniture, wood carvings, and seventeenth-, eighteenth-, and nineteenth-century religious paintings. These came from the Jesuit mission of Miraflores in Salta and from Peru and Bolivia. The house also displays books and documents of historical value and archeological artifacts found on the estate.

Molinos
Luracatao
Bodegas Colomé
La Angostura

For almost three hundred years, the present-day hostelry in the village of Molinos was the main house of a *finca* that administered a large number of estates in the Calchaquí Valleys in the western part of the province of Salta. In its colonial heyday, when cattle were driven for sale across the high Andean passes to Chile, Molinos was ideally located along the trade route.

At the time of the Spanish conquest, the valleys were home to several Diaguitas tribes, who were both industrious and warlike. While the former quality was indis-

Left: Molinos's old sala was recently restored and turned into an inn. Its rooms have been simply and colorfully decorated with pots and other ancient artifacts found in the area as well as with carpets and wall hangings woven locally on rustic looms. The sofa upholstery is also the work of local artisans.

Right: The utter simplicity of the design and materials gives this courtyard and roofed veranda a timeless charm. The blue-painted posts have been hewn into rustic columns. Square in shape and enclosed all around, the patio is characteristic of the region.

pensable to the new masters' plan of subjugation, the latter was to give rise to a hundred-year struggle between the two sides. History singles out Juan Calchaquí as a valiant cacique; among the notable Spanish captains was Diego Díez Gómez. In the 1680s his services to the Crown were rewarded with an encomienda of local Indians. To make full use of the slave labor of the vanquished, he set up a cattle ranch, naming it San Pedro Nolasco de los Molinos de Calchaquí. In return for their "two lifetimes" of labor, it was his duty to instruct the Indians in the Christian faith and to provide them with land and water for cultivating crops. Díez Gómez was succeeded by his daughter, Magdalena; as she died childless, her estate and privileges went to her second husband, General Domingo de Isasi Isasmendi. Many of the current owners of the *fincas* that were once part of a twenty-seven-thousand-square-mile estate are descendants of the general and his second wife. Molinos became the general's favorite residence, and he died there—in what is now the inn—in 1767.

Nicolás Severo de Isasmendi, the general's eldest son, inherited the property and he, too, served the Crown well. In 1781 he helped put down the revolt of the Indians under Tupac Amaru. Don Nicolás was the last royal governor of Salta, and during

Left: The interior of the village church has a number of baroque elements—the pulpit, its canopy, and the large, two-tiered altarpiece—but the underlying feeling is of naive wonderment.

Right: The village turns out for the procession of the Virgin of the Valley. The church is eighteenth century, yet its understated facade and towers—a far cry from the sophistication of Jesuit architects— tell of a simple faith. The decoration at the four corners of the domed towers finds a counterpart in the finials crowning the gate piers and fence posts that enclose the terraced churchyard.

Molinos · Luracatao · Bodegas Colomé · La Angostura   165

the 1810 revolution for independence the Calchaquí Valleys remained loyal to Spain. But even with the political change his prestige was respected. He remarried in 1811, at the age of fifty-eight, and died twenty-six years later, leaving his children a huge legacy. His mummified body can be seen in the Molinos church.

In 1837 Nicolás's widow sold the Calchaquí estate to Indalecio Gómez, who a short while later bought Pampa Grande from the family of General Arenales. It was a period of intense economic activity, with wine production and traffic in mules and cattle to Chile and Bolivia. The estate's warehouses had stores of maize, wheat, jerked beef, goat- and sheepskins, gourds, and cheeses. This prosperity was interrupted only by the assassination of Gómez in 1863, when civil war raged in the valleys. Then, early in the twentieth century, the routes of commerce changed, and Molinos went into decline. For many years, the house, with its spacious rooms and immense courtyards, and the vast granaries lay abandoned.

The idea to convert the old house into an inn came in 1971 as part of a plan to promote tourism in Salta. The restoration, paid for by provincial and national funding, took eight years and was headed up by architect Ana Iturrieta de Cruz. Original features—the stone foundations, adobe walls, woven-reed ceilings, and beams of *cardón*, a common cactus of the cordillera—were retained. But the tiled floors were relaid with flagstone and the old mud-and-straw roof, a construction that requires periodic renewal, was replaced with tiles. At the same time, five of the house's six courtyards have been kept. One had been the owner's, another contained an *algarrobo* tree and bread oven; bedrooms had opened onto the third; the stableyard housed a

Left: Llamas, seen here in a pen at Luracatao, are a domestic animal no longer known in the wild. They are closely related to guanacos, alpacas, and vicuñas. The Incas used the llama for its meat and wool and as a beast of burden. The wool comes in a variety of colors and is still woven into ponchos in the Salta valleys; one characteristic of the animal is that the tips of its ears turn in.

Right: The humble thatched adobe hut of a valley dweller is not unlike the first ranchos that served as homesteads for early settlers everywhere in Argentina. Under the vivid blue vault of the sky, this structure is in perfect harmony with the harsh landscape.

168 Salta Province

Left: Entrance gate to the sala *of Luracatao, flanked by two specimens of a large cactus (Trichocereus terscheckii) commonly known as the* cardón *and plentiful in the area.*

Right: The cabinet here in the living room was made on the finca *from the wood of its own trees.*

candle works and other domestic industries; and the last, just around the corner from the church, was the courtyard of the servants' quarters.

Luracatao, named for the Indian tribe that once inhabited the region, is situated in the high valleys of western Salta, 43 miles from the village of Molinos. The *finca* has been in the Isasmendi family for 250 years.

In the early days, when the estate measured over 90 miles from north to south, it counted some 600 head of cattle, as well as horses, sheep, and several dozen mules. The *finca* also produced alpaca, guanaco, and vicuña wools for its own consumption. In the last century and the beginning of this, young cattle were fattened on alfalfa before they were driven over 13,000-foot passes to be sold in Chile.

Don Robustiano Patrón Costas—married to doña Elisea Ortiz Isasmendi— provided the *finca* with new drive in the 1930s when he began breeding shorthorn cattle, merino and Romney Marsh rams, and Peruvian horses. Margarita Patrón Costas de López Lecube, their daughter, is Luracatao's present owner. Her son, Enrique López Lecube, now runs the estate. He has modernized the seventeenth-century *sala*, cutting down the number of rooms but preserving the almost monastic austerity of its original style. Locally woven textiles ornament the interior decor. Among these are carpets that mix modern and traditional colors and designs.

The *finca* contains nearly 7,000 square miles, divided between mountains and valleys, and is inhabited by 3,000 people, who live mainly in 4 villages. Each settlement has its own school, health facilities, and in some cases a chapel. The schoolchildren number 600. A large part of the arable land, which for generations was rented to local farmers, has been sold to them. The remaining 4,000 arable acres are now under the estate's direct management. The area is especially good for

PAGES 170–71
High above the valley among cardones, *goats nibble at the leaves of shrubs and stunted trees.*

172   Salta Province

Left: Here, amid an awe-inspiring landscape over 6,500 feet up in the arid hills near La Angostura, a flock of sheep and a goat graze among the boulders.

Right: Red peppers, harvested in March, dry in the sun before being taken to the mill for grinding. They were introduced into the Calchaquí Valleys in the mid-1930s, when it became impossible to import them from Spain.

growing lavender and pimiento, which blankets the hills in red. The mountains rimming the valley rise to peaks of over 16,000 feet, and much of the terrain resembles a moonscape. Here, where only a few shepherds live, mule tracks thread sheer precipices and the air is so thin it causes mountain sickness.

Although Catholics, the inhabitants of the Calchaquí Valleys still worship Pachamama, the earth mother of Andean Indians. They also believe in the mythical Coquena, protectress of wild fauna, especially the vicuña. Amid such mountains—the highest in the world outside the Himalayas—it is easy to imagine the awe and fear in which early man held nature.

Bodegas Colomé, which is a winery, and La Angostura, a horse-breeding ranch, are establishments some 6,500 feet up in the Calchaquí Valleys in the western part of the department of Molinos. The Colomé River supplies the water that irrigates the *finca* bearing its name. Owing to the sunlight it enjoys—strong even at the coldest time of year—the land has proved singularly apt for the cultivation of grapes and other fruits.

These estates were part of Nicolás Severo's legacy to his daughter, Ascención Isasmendi. After the death of her husband, José Benjamín Dávalos, who was governor of Salta and died in office in 1867, Ascención set out to make wine production in the valleys a commercial venture. Until then it had been little more than a cottage industry. Importing quality French grapes, she won a gold medal for her wines at the first exposition of the industry in Argentina, held in Córdoba in 1871.

Her descendants grew other crops—pimientos, cumin, and anise—but the estate's aim at present is to increase its wine-making capacity. Viñas de Dávalos is the name under which its wines are sold. The *finca*'s red varieties are Cabernet and Malbec; its white is Torrontés. These wines are marketed in Salta, Buenos Aires, and Paris.

The horses raised at La Angostura are a Peruvian breed of trotter. They have been exhibited with great success in Buenos Aires at the annual Palermo show.

Left: Snowy peaks tower above the Colomé vineyard, whose temperate climate makes for a delicately aromatic wine. Malbec, one of the red varieties grown here, is the most widely cultivated grape in Argentina.

Right: The wine is stored in wooden casks above ground in an ancient shed with a high, woven-reed ceiling. Torrontés, the white wine produced at Colomé, is described as having "a flowery, perfumed nose and dry, pithy, orange fruit on the palate."

Below: An old wine press, standing on a millstone, ornaments the patio under a spreading aguaribay, or pepper tree (Schinus molle), a native evergreen species grown as a shade tree. The Torrontés grape was brought to Salta from the Canary Islands in the 1550s.

Molinos · Luracatao · Bodegas Colomé · La Angostura   175

La Primavera
Arroyo Verde

Along the Chilean border in the southern Andes, over eight hundred miles southwest of Buenos Aires, lies Argentina's spectacular lake district, an immense territory of snow-capped peaks, glaciers, and primeval forests. Two adjoining national parks—Lanín and Nahuel Huapi—have been set aside for the protection and promotion of this area of outstanding natural beauty. Nahuel Huapi, occupying over three thousand square miles, straddles two provinces—the extreme south of Neuquén and the west of Río Negro. Within the latter reserve is a small third park, Los Arrayanes, named for a rare indigenous tree of the myrtle family that grows there on a peninsula jutting out into Lake Nahuel Huapi.

The region is also ethnologically rich. It was a last stronghold of the Araucanians, who, after the Diaguitas, were the most civilized of the Indians living in what is now Argentina. Their archeological remains can be found throughout the area, including painted rocks—outdoors and in caves—that bear intriguing geometrical designs and

Left: La Primavera's dining room is furnished in a traditional English style. Reflecting one of the owners' passions, the French porcelain plates are decorated with fishing flies.

Right: The family's interest in the outdoors is also revealed in the entrance hall, which displays the antlers of a red deer, an introduced species, and prints of local fauna by Axel Amuchástegui, Argentina's foremost animal painter. The tapestry-covered sofa is seventeenth-century English.

Left: Built in 1924, the house later had an upper floor added to it, when a new slate roof imported from Belgium replaced the original corrugated iron. In a setting of mountain and forest, the wood siding and ample entrance porch—both in Chilean cedar—give La Primavera the appropriate look of a hunting lodge.

Right: The estancia's old triple-roofed barn, used for storing hay and keeping animals in winter, is protected from the region's frequent strong winds by stately poplars. La Primavera was founded by an American dentist who went broke when a gigantic flock of his sheep was lost in a snowstorm while being driven over the mountains to Chile.

symbols. Topographical names all over the two provinces abound in Araucanian words: *leufú*—"river"; *lauquén*—"lake"; *nahuel huapi*—"tiger island." As late as 1880, the rawhide tents of the Araucanian caciques Inacayal and Sayhueque still dotted the shores of Andean lakes. Their people grew wheat and maize, gathered the edible seed of the araucaria tree, and traded with both the Tehuelches of southern Patagonia and whites from Carmen de Patagones on the Atlantic shore. Travelers praised the refinement of these caciques, their melodious language, the politeness with which they served their guests alcoholic beverages, and the long parliaments in which they discussed problems of tribal interest.

One of the district's major lakes and a noted paradise for salmon fishermen is Traful ("big water" in the aboriginal language). Out of it flows the Traful River, swift and clear, over a boulder-strewn bed to the broad Limay and the Río Negro, on a five-hundred-mile journey to the sea. The picturesque Traful Valley is the site of the Larivière family's two estancias, La Primavera and Arroyo Verde, each containing about fifteen thousand acres. La Primavera ("springtime"), the original property, is on the south side of the river and belongs to Felipe Larivière; Arroyo Verde (named for the nearby brook that flows into the Traful), on the north side, belongs to Mauricio Larivière.

In Argentine history, the settlement of Patagonia is a late event. The conquistadors first blundered into the area in search of a fabled city of gold. The true explorers were the Jesuit fathers who came as missionaries in the seventeenth and eighteenth centuries, Thomas Falkner among them. Then in the last century came a new breed of explorer-adventurer, typified by men like Francisco P. Moreno and George Chaworth Musters, author of *At Home with the Patagonians*. Moreno, who wrote several books about the area (in one he mentions his three crossings of the Traful), was a member of a commission to establish the Chilean-Argentine boundary. In 1903 he gave the government the three square leagues of land that became the nucleus of Nahuel Huapi National Park.

Above: At Arroyo Verde rustic tables are laid for an Argentine asado, or barbecue, on a pebbled terrace that overlooks Lake Traful.

Right: A guest cabin is nestled among wind-blasted trees on a rocky cliff above the lake. The estancia is located in Nahuel Huapi National Park in the southern Andes.

Around the turn of the century the government began to sell ten-thousand-hectare sections of land in order to encourage settlement of the area. Buyers had to occupy, fence in, and improve the land. The offer attracted many foreign investors who wished to become ranchers. An American, George Newbery—uncle of Argentina's famous pioneer aviator—was one of them. In 1906 he bought land on the Traful River and, after ruthlessly running off squatters, built La Primavera's first house and sheds. Devoted to large-scale sheep raising, the establishment changed hands in 1923. Its new owner was Sir Henry Bell, an Englishman, president of Argentina's Southern Railways and of a company with other large estates in the area. Attracted to the Traful for its beauty, Bell imported pedigreed cows and sheep and in summer pastured his herds and flocks fifty-two hundred feet up in the Andean foothills. The new house he erected was a big, single-story chalet built of local stone, with a porch at the front and a corrugated iron roof. The same structure, with the addition of an upper floor and a blue slate roof, makes up the present-day *casco* of La Primavera. Sir Henry, however, was not happy. When his much younger wife fell in love with a nearby rancher, Bell quit the estancia, leaving it in the hands of a majordomo who decided to take advantage of the incipient tourism that the new railroad was bringing to Nahuel Huapi. La Primavera was converted into a pleasant hotel, one of whose guests was British World War I hero Lord Allenby. Among others attracted to the river for the salmon fishing have been President Eisenhower, King Leopold of

*Left: This handsome bar and rough-hewn plank wall are fashioned of the richly colored local Chilean cedar (*Austrocedrus chilensis*), one of Nahuel Huapi Park's most common and important trees.*

*Right: Comfortable and informal, Arroyo Verde was built in 1976 of stone and of the native Chilean cedar (locally known as ciprés) and is set in a magnificent garden that contains a wide variety of shrubs and flowers. Another conifer of the zone is the source of the shingles on the roof—*Fitzyroya cupressoides*. The national park has three-thousand-year-old specimens of this slow-growing giant, whose diameter reaches ten feet.*

PAGES 184–85
Hereford cattle is the breed that best adapts to the rigors of this part of Patagonia. Here, in preparation for branding, animals are roped with a lasso. Elsewhere in Argentina—on the pampa, especially—a chute is more commonly used when working with cattle.

Left: Evening sunlight floods the eroded heights of these Andean foothills, which lie within the estancia's perimeters. Much of the landscape hereabouts was shaped by the action of glacial ice.

Right: Argentina's glorious lake district, with its bracing air, virgin forests, and spectacular views, preserves a primeval tang. Here in the Traful River and in nearby streams and lakes are brook, rainbow, and brown trout as well as the only landlocked salmon in all South America.

Belgium, and the Infanta Cristina of Spain as well as such renowned angling authors as Roderick Haig-Brown, Joe Brooks, and Ernest Schwiebert.

In the summer of 1932 a Franco-Argentine diplomat, Felipe Larivière, visited with his wife and children. The family was escaping the strictures of mourning as it was practiced at the time. Instead of spending the summer at fashionable Mar del Plata, they chose Nahuel Huapi as a spot little frequented by people from Buenos Aires. Larivière was so enthusiastic about the place that he reserved the hotel for himself for two seasons running. Then, in 1936, he journeyed to England, where he talked the now retired Bell into selling him his Neuquén estate. Over the next forty years, La Primavera's new proprietor, who also owned other land in the province of Buenos Aires, used the estancia almost exclusively for his recreation. After his death in 1975, his sons Mauricio and Felipe divided the estate. Mauricio took his share in land, with river and lake access, and he and his wife, Mémé, had to build a house and outbuildings on the property. Stag and boar have been introduced into the area, and condors can be seen in the cordillera. Other native fauna include a wide variety of waterfowl and the silent puma. Snow-covered peaks are visible from the terrace of the main house and from the picturesque cabin on a cliff that descends straight down to the lake. In spring wildflowers are plentiful, while in autumn the landscape is ablaze with the golden foliage of the southern beech.

María Behety

Ferdinand Magellan in 1520 was the first white man to set eyes on Tierra del Fuego, the large island south of Patagonia and the famous straits he discovered. On the shore he saw the smoke of many fires, which may have been lit as a warning by the Ona aborigines. He called his discovery "Fireland." When in December 1832 the *Beagle*, with Darwin aboard, approached the channel that had been named after the ship, his first descriptive words were "rugged" and "inhospitable." "Tierra del Fuego," he went on to write, "may be described as a mountainous country, partly submerged in the sea, so that deep islets and bays occupy the place where valleys should exist."

Bleak and windswept, a forbidding and terrifying wilderness, this southern tip of the continent is a vast archipelago of islands divided arbitrarily between Argentina and Chile and located fifteen hundred miles from Buenos Aires. It is an epic territory that stirs all our imaginations, a place where within barely a hundred years a series of missionaries, sheep farmers, and government officials brought a whole race of Indians to extinction.

When José Menéndez, a Spanish immigrant (via Cuba, Montevideo, Buenos Aires, and Punta Arenas in nearby Chile), bought land by public auction in the 1890s for his second estancia in Tierra del Fuego, he described the terrain as "without mountains or high peaks, tangled forests, peat bogs, or arid plateaus." This was not Darwin's Tierra del Fuego but the middle of a plain in the part of the island north of the Río Grande. Menéndez had explored the area on horseback five years earlier when he had decided to expand his activities from the Chilean to the Argentine side

Left: The very magnitude of María Behety's shearing shed reflects the role and scale of sheep farming in the far south of Argentina, where Corriedales—first imported from New Zealand in 1905—are the leading breed. Argentina ranks fifth in the world in sheep production.

Right: Constant high winds, especially from the west and south, are the chief feature of the weather in these latitudes. Where poplars will not grow, as here, picket fences, sometimes ten feet high, are employed as windbreaks to protect crops and buildings. This one, surrounding María Behety's park, sports decorative windows.

PAGES 190–91
The main buildings, where up to 150 people work and live, form an isolated prairie community that strives for self-sufficiency. Often estancias like this will have their own private planes, airstrips, and hangars.

From top to bottom, respectively, the bakery, shepherds' quarters, and farmhands' kitchen—all straightforward constructions clad and roofed in the corrugated-iron sheets that are ubiquitous in Tierra del Fuego. The work force here is made up primarily of Chileans.

of the frontier. His first Argentine estancia, La Primera Argentina, south of the Río Grande, measured 540 square miles; his later acquisition, La Segunda Argentina, the biggest, best, and most valuable of Menéndez's holdings in Tierra del Fuego, covered nearly 700 square miles.

Within a few years, José Menéndez proved that it was possible to graze one sheep per hectare (nearly 2½ acres), and his Tierra del Fuego establishments became models of their kind. La Segunda Argentina was divided into three stations, Miranda, El Castillo, and María Behety, each with a house, sheep dip, and required outbuildings. One of these, a shearing shed—said to be among the largest in the world—handled 140,000 sheep at a rate of 7,000 a day.

Menéndez had arrived in Punta Arenas in 1876. It was a troubled period in the territory's settlement, an era of ruthless adventurers and gold prospectors such as the legendary Julius Popper. By the end of the century the Argentine and Chilean governments had sold or leased Indian land to missionaries and white sheep farmers. The Ona, guanaco hunters from the north of the island, and Yahgans (or Yamana), who fished the Beagle Channel, were forced "for their own protection" to seek refuge with Salesian fathers at the former mission of La Candelaria, north of the town of Río Grande, but there, cooped up, they died of disease and heartbreak. Otherwise the Indians were relentlessly hunted down and exterminated by farm managers, who held that the aboriginals made poor farmhands and, what was worse, were not averse to helping themselves to the sheep of others. One Scottish sheepman, Alexander MacLennan, known as the Red Pig, was recruited to exterminate Indians, and he offered one pound sterling for every Indian ear brought to him. But there were also men like Thomas Bridges, who made Harberton, his estancia on the Beagle Channel, a refuge for Indians. Bridges spent a lifetime compiling a Yamana-English dictionary, about which Bruce Chatwin wrote in his book on Patagonia: "The *Dictionary* survived the Indians to become their monument." Bridges's son Lucas was the author of the classic account of Tierra del Fuego, *Uttermost Part of the Earth*. The last pure Ona male died in 1969.

After José Menéndez's death in 1918, his children formed the Sociedad Anónima Ganadera Argentina. They also changed the name of La Primera Argentina to José Menéndez and La Segunda to María Behety, in honor of Menéndez's wife. In 1953 this latter estancia, with its *casco* and 43,000 hectares, became the property of Carlos Menéndez Behety, the founder's son. His children and grandchildren are the present owners of the estate, which supports 43,000 Corriedale sheep and 1,300 Hereford cattle.

The *casco* has all the typical features of Fuegian and Patagonian estancias. It is fitted out for hard winters, great snows, and ceaseless winds, and everything necessary for survival is provided: a school, health clinic, greenhouses for garden vegetables, an electricity-generating plant, library, slaughterhouse, cookhouse, quarters for shearers, shepherds, and laborers, kennels, stables, bathhouse, and bakery.

The owner's house at María Behety has suffered the usual ravages of the climate. The first dwelling, which had been imported from Europe and was made of wood, burned to the ground in 1922. A roomy, well-heated masonry residence replaced it. In 1988 it, too, burned down. The open grassland in the north of Tierra del Fuego offers no protection from the inhospitable winds, and extensive windbreaks have had to be erected on estancias that by necessity must house up to 150 people in settlements that amount to tiny villages. With heavy winds and wooden houses heated by stoves, there is an ever-present hazard of fire, which is why an estancia's buildings tend to be spread out.

La Cristina

Patagonia proper begins at the Río Negro, five hundred miles south of Buenos Aires, and, according to some, runs all the way to Cape Horn. Those who live in Tierra del Fuego prefer being called Fuegians rather than Patagonians, holding that Patagonia ends at the Strait of Magellan. This vast, underpopulated territory—the present-day provinces of Río Negro, Chubut, and Santa Cruz—is an arid plateau cut by a number of broad, flat-bottomed valleys. The rivers all flow eastward from the Andes and empty themselves in the South Atlantic. According to legend, Magellan's chronicler saw a giant Tehuelche Indian dancing naked on the shore. From the size of his moccasins, Magellan dubbed him *Patagón*—"Big Foot."

Stock raising is a major industry throughout Patagonia. Río Negro Province is also renowned for fruit orchards that produce 72 percent of Argentina's apples. And to the south, in Chubut and Santa Cruz, there is oil, gas, and mining. But as Bruce Chatwin noted in his book *In Patagonia*, "As you go south down the coast, the grass gets greener, the sheep farms richer and the British more numerous. They are the sons and grandsons of the men who cleared and fenced the land in the 1890s."

Santa Cruz was settled late and is still the country's most thinly populated province. Around the turn of the century the number of pioneers who had braved the Patagonian solitude were easily countable. In addition to the British, people came from Germany, the Balkans, Spain, and the Falkland Islands to found estancias. Falkland sheep were brought over and other flocks were driven south from Río Negro. Land was cheaper in Santa Cruz but was far from ports and exposed to the rigors of a harsh climate.

Left: Snow coats a picket fence at La Cristina. Hesketh Prichard, a Scot, searching for a prehistoric monster, named the Catarina River in 1901 and was the first man to explore this extremely remote valley. Thirteen years later an English couple founded the estancia as a sheep ranch.

Right: Inching down into Lake Argentino, the Upsala Glacier forms one of the estancia's boundaries. Here, where nature works on a colossal scale and towering ice fields extend north for over four hundred miles, the Chileans and Argentines have long disputed the frontier. The latter pressed for a line that connected the highest peaks; the former preferred the Pacific-Atlantic divide. Each country's stand favored itself.

Few of the early settlers ventured beyond the arid coastal plateau into the lake district along the Chilean frontier. That vast lakeland was isolated, almost inaccessible, but water was abundant and the grazing rich. Among those tempted by this out-of-the-way land was Josef Percival Masters. Born in England, he and his English wife of Norwegian ancestry first lived at an estancia called El Cóndor, forty miles from the town of Río Gallegos in the very south of the province. In 1902 their son Percival Herbert was born there by the Strait of Magellan.

Masters later moved to Calafate, a couple of hundred miles northwest, on the shore of Lake Argentino. Hearing from some pathfinders that fertile glacial valleys were to be found at the far end of the lake, he set off by boat in search of a suitable place to set up a sheep farm. The region at the foot of the Upsala Glacier immediately attracted him. Its valleys were dotted with small glacier lakes and protected by high mountains. Masters chose a broad valley close to the point where the Catarina River flowed into the northern tip of forty-seven-mile-long Lake Argentino. His valley was set off by snow-capped mountains on whose lower slopes grew the ñire, the so-called low beech of the southern Andes. Used for timber, in autumn its leaves turn a variety of reds, yellows, and browns. The lakes were inhabited by ducks, flamingoes, upland geese, black-necked swans, and ibises; overhead flew birds of prey, such as the caracara, the chimango, and the enormous condor, with its wingspread of over nine feet. There were also red fox, wildcats, pumas, and guanacos. You sometimes came upon the guanacos' dying place, where five hundred of them might be piled one on top of another, decaying.

La Cristina was built in 1914. It covered an area of twenty-five thousand hectares

La Cristina's orchard grew apples, pears, cherries, and plums, and there was a well-tended kitchen garden. Everything was manufactured on the estancia—boots, carpets, furniture, and clothes. A good radio kept the Masters family in touch with the world, especially in winter, when outdoor work was impossible. These humble buildings with their poplar windbreaks stand today as testimony of man's indomitable courage in the face of privation and hardship.

The estancia's inhabitants and its fleeces crossed the lake's milky-blue waters in this boat. The journey was always potentially hazardous. Icebergs the size of cathedrals plunge off the glacier face, unleashing tidal waves, and the ferocious weather often whips up white breakers.

(nearly one hundred square miles), and in its peak years had twenty thousand sheep. The Upsala Glacier, a three-hour journey from the *casco* on horseback, formed one of the estancia's boundaries. As the establishment could only be approached by water, it was necessary to navigate the thirty miles between Puerto Bandera and the quiet bay where the estancia is located. To this day, great caution must be exercised on the lake. Bergs breaking off the glaciers' nearly two-hundred-foot-high ice walls make an ear-splitting din and cause huge waves. The lake is also subject to sudden violent squalls.

In his novel *Lago Argentino*, published in 1946, the Argentine writer Juan Goyanarte described the glaciers and ice this way: "The icebergs of frozen seas, floating nine-tenths underwater and one-tenth above, are heavy and clumsy. The icebergs of Lake Argentino are just the opposite. Their smallest part in the water, the rest above the surface, they are at the whim of the wind, like flecks of foam. These are no ordinary ice blocks formed by freezing water but are of an older, blue-blooded ancestry. They are made only of snow that fell on high summits several millenia ago . . . [to form] a great serpent of frothy ice on a centuries-long march to the lake."

In 1933 the land that made up La Cristina became part of the immense Glaciers National Park, and today the establishment no longer functions as a sheep farm. Its houses, stables, and the old shearing shed are clad in corrugated iron. They, as well as the furniture and the boat once used to transport wool, were all built from the wood of trees growing on the estancia. La Cristina continues to be the home of Janet McDonald Masters, the eighty-two-year-old widow of the founder's son.

Selected Bibliography

Nineteenth Century

Darwin, Charles. *Voyage of the* Beagle. First published in 1839 as the third volume of Robert FitzRoy's account of the *Beagle* voyage and subsequently under a number of different titles.

Head, Francis Bond. *Rough Notes Taken During Some Rapid Journeys Across the Pampas and Among the Andes*. London: John Murray, 1826. Reprint. Carbondale and Edwardsville: Southern Illinois University Press, 1967.

Hudson, W.H. *The Naturalist in La Plata*. 1892. Reprint. London: J. M. Dent, 1923.

————. *Idle Days in Patagonia*. 1893. Reprint. London: J. M. Dent, 1923.

Hutchinson, Thomas J. *The Parana; with Incidents of the Paraguayan War and South American Recollections from 1861 to 1868*. London: Edward Stanford, 1868.

MacCann, William. *Two Thousand Miles' Ride through the Argentine Provinces*. 2 vols. London: Smith, Elder, 1853.

Parish, Sir Woodbine. *Buenos Aires, and the Provinces of the Rio de la Plata*. London: John Murray, 1839; enl. ed., 1852.

Sarmiento, Domingo Faustino. *Life in the Argentine Republic in the Days of the Tyrants; or, Civilization and Barbarism*. New York: Hurd and Houghton, 1868. Reprint. New York: Hafner Press, 1972.

Twentieth Century

Abad de Santillán, Diego. *Historia argentina*. 5 vols. Buenos Aires: Tipográfica Editora Argentina, 1965–71.

————. *Diccionario de argentinismos de ayer y de hoy*. Buenos Aires: Tipográfica Editora Argentina, 1976.

Assunçao, Fernando O. *El gaucho: estudio socio-cultural*. 2 vols. Montevideo: Dirección general de extensión universitaria, 1978–79.

————. *Pilchas criollas: usos y costumbres del gaucho*. Montevideo: Ediciones Master Fer, 1979.

Barreto, Margarita. *El mate: su historia y cultura*. Buenos Aires: Ediciones del Sol and Ediciones de Aquí a la Vuelta, 1989.

Bridges, Lucas. *Uttermost Part of the Earth*. 1948. Reprint. London: Century, 1987.

Brown, Jonathan C. *A Socioeconomic History of Argentina, 1776–1860*. London: Cambridge University Press, 1979.

Cabrera, Angel, and José Yepes. *Mamíferos sudamericanos*. 2 vols. Buenos Aires: Ediar Editores, 1960.

Chatwin Bruce. *In Patagonia*. London: Jonathan Cape, 1977.

Cunninghame Graham, R. B. *Thirty Tales and Sketches*. London: Duckworth, 1929.

————. *Rodeo*. London: William Heinemann, 1936.

————. *The Essential R. B. Cunninghame Graham*. London: Jonathan Cape, 1952.

————. *The South American Sketches of R. B. Cunninghame Graham*. Norman, Okla.: University of Oklahoma Press, 1978.

Glusberg, Jorge. *Breve historia de la arquitectura argentina*. 2 vols. Buenos Aires: Editorial Claridad, 1991.

Graham-Yooll, Andrew. *The Forgotten Colony: A History of the English-Speaking Communities in Argentina*. London: Hutchinson, 1981.

Hudson, W.H. *El Ombú*. 1902. Reprint. London: J. M. Dent, 1923.

————. *Far Away and Long Ago: A History of My Early Life*. 1918. Reprint. London: J. M. Dent, 1923.

————. *Birds of La Plata*. 1920. Reprint. London: J. M. Dent, 1923.

Martínez Estrada, Ezequiel. *X-Ray of the Pampa*. Austin: University of Texas Press, 1972.

Molina, Enrique, and Angel Bonomini. *Molina Campos*. Buenos Aires: Asociación Amigos de las Artes Tradicionales, 1989.

Molinari, Ricardo Luis. *Biografía de la pampa*. Buenos Aires: Ediciones de Arte Gaglianone, 1987.

Narosky, T., and D. Yzurieta. *Guía para la identificación de las aves de Argentina y Uruguay*. Buenos Aires: Vázquez Mazzini Editores, 1987.

————. *El país de los argentinos*. 4 vols. Buenos Aires: Centro Editor de América Latina, 1975–76.

Sáenz, Justo P. (h). *Equitación gaucha en la pampa y Mesopotamia*. Buenos Aires: Ediciones Peuser, 1951.

Sáenz Quesada, María. *Los estancieros*. Buenos Aires: Editorial de Belgrano, 1981.

Saubidet, Tito. *Pequeño vocabulario y refranero criollo*. Buenos Aires: Sainte Claire Editora, 1988.

Tschiffely, A. F. *This Way Southward: An Account of a Journey through Patagonia to Tierra del Fuego*. London: Hodder & Stoughton, 1946.

Glossary

By now, some 450-odd years since the pampa was first settled by Europeans, terms specific to the Argentine countryside are worth whole specialized dictionaries and handbooks. Because rural Argentina has become so thoroughly mythologized and because many basic words are so distant from their original meanings, ordinary Argentines themselves are often unclear or confused about terms they hear and use every day. What follows, however, is a brief guide addressed primarily to English-speaking readers.

Casco. The *casco* of an estancia is the part that contains the various dwellings of its overseers (a *majordomo*, or administrator, who was not the owner, and a *capataz*, or foreman, who directed work) and hands, together with its outbuildings—barns, toolsheds, open-sided cattle sheds, etc.—and its corrals, vegetable gardens, and woods (see pages 79–80). In other words, the nucleus of the estancia, as distinct from its surrounding open rangeland. Today the word *casco* is more popularly and narrowly used to mean the estancia's main house—that of its proprietor and his family, when they are in residence. *Casco*, in Spanish, means "head" or "skull" and is also used to denote the center of a town as distinct from its environs. Starting from scratch today, no one would build an estancia and place its livestock and working areas cheek by jowl with dwellings. When Argentine estancias were first founded at the end of the sixteenth century, however—and nearly to the end of the nineteenth century—a prime concern of their layout was defensive.

Estancia. To any Argentine, country- or city-born, of old stock or a recent immigrant, the word *estancia* is part of the national consciousness—that is, part real, part myth, and part pure nostalgia. The word derives from the verb *estar*, "to be," not in the existential sense but in the meaning of position, location, or placement—"to stand," "to be stationed"—hence its early meaning as a grant of land of a particular size for use in grazing cattle. The present-day meaning of a rural establishment for the raising of livestock, principally cattle, came later. By extension, the *estancia* also refers to whatever buildings or other constructions belong to such an establishment. Charles Darwin, during his extensive travels in the Argentine in the 1830s, translated the word in a footnote as "farm estate." The term "station," as currently used in the Australian outback and New Zealand for a stock farm, had its origin at this same time and is an exact equivalent. The corresponding term in the far west of the United States is "ranch," a word that came into English around 1831 via Mexico, where the Spanish *rancho*—meaning

"hut" or "hovel," as it still does in the Argentine—was a small farm.

Gaucho. The gaucho came to be the great River Plate horseman and drover, expert in working with livestock and skilled in handling the lasso, the bolas, and the knife—the basic instruments of his work. His origins, however, are as obscure and controversial as the root of the word *gaucho* itself. The product of a racial mix between Indians, blacks, and the first Spaniards, the gaucho in colonial times was a nomad who lived on the margins of society—that is, he lived freely on the pampa as a cattle thief. It was the age of hides, and attempts were made by the authorities to control the slaughter of herds. According to one historian, eighteen or twenty gauchos hunting wild cows with sharp, sicklelike blades attached to long poles—with which the cattle's hind tendons were severed—could fell seven or eight hundred animals in an hour. Money was to be made from such "cattle mining," as this illicit trade was then called. The range, however, was unending, unowned, and unfenced, and cattle and horses multiplied and roamed wild. This situation gave impetus to the *gaucho malo*, or outlaw. Hence, in time the word *gaucho* became a synonym for "ne'er-do-well," "robber," or even "murderer." After the outset of the revolution against Spain, in which the gaucho was to make an indispensable contribution, attitudes slowly changed and there even grew up a whole genre—*literatura gauchesca*—in prose and verse, in which gaucho life was described, aggrandized, and ultimately turned into myth. Some of this writing was purely picturesque, much of it descended into sentimentality and may be looked on as another example of the cult of the noble savage, but the best of this work, by writers like Bartolomé Hidalgo, Hilario Ascasubi, Estanislao del Campo, and José Hernández, has real merit. Hernández's *Martín Fierro*—its two parts date, respectively, from 1872 and 1879—is deservedly the Argentine national epic. A novel in verse, it is at once an exciting tale and an eloquent defense of the gaucho, alienated from the society of his day. To the poet Ascasubi, writing in the middle of the last century, the gaucho most often was "poor, but he is free and, owing to his very poverty and his few needs, independent; he is hospitable at home, full of keen intelligence and shrewdness, physically agile, short on words, vigorous and circumspect in his actions, guarded when he speaks to outsiders, with a poetic and superstitious tinge to his beliefs and speech, and extraordinarily skilled in traveling alone over the immense Argentine deserts, securing for himself food, horses, and so forth, with his lasso and bolas." Domingo F. Sarmiento, the nineteenth-

century writer, statesman, and champion of civilized values, praised the gaucho for his intimate knowledge of the country, pointing out the incredible skill of the *rastreador*, or track finder, whose work it was "to follow a horse's tracks, and to distinguish them among a thousand others, and to know whether it was going at an easy or a rapid pace, at liberty or led, laden or carrying no weight" and of the *baqueano*, or pathfinder, who would know every span of twenty thousand square leagues of flat terrain and be able to guide a traveler over the featureless plain to a place fifty leagues away or to announce the approach of an enemy up to ten leagues off, while at shorter distances "he notices the clouds of dust, and estimates the number of the hostile force by their density." But Sarmiento also recognized the gaucho as a "white-skinned savage, at war with society and proscribed by the laws" and consequently held him responsible in part for the primitiveness and bloody strife that afflicted the fledgling republic throughout the nineteenth century. It was the hapless gaucho who made up the rabble armies of the despotic caudillos—men like López, Ramírez, Artigas, Quiroga, Urquiza, and the blood-stained Rosas—who ruthlessly held sway over the Argentine provinces as if they were their own private fiefdoms. Darwin, meeting this gaucho cavalry for the first time on one of their expeditions to exterminate Indians, noted: "I should think such a villanous, banditti-like army, was never before collected together." The gaucho disappeared, or was assimilated, after the range was divided and fenced in the last century. His descendants are the *paisanos* who populate rural Argentina today, and the word *gauchada*—an act or action appropriate to a gaucho—no longer stands for "wiliness" and "meanness" as it once did but became "a manly act," one carried out with boldness and skill. While to some Argentines the gaucho is a heroic symbol for lost freedom and untrammeled nature, to others he touches off unsavory sentiments of jingoism and lawlessness, such as the utter contempt with which the army held the rule of law in the Argentine Republic for most of the past half century. Readers of English will find the pages of W. H. Hudson filled with firsthand knowledge of gaucho life. There is also valuable gaucho lore in certain passages of the work of R. B. Cunninghame Graham.

Hacienda. In the southwestern United States (and to anyone who has seen a Western film), this is a ranch or farm or farm dwelling. In parts of Argentina the word means the same thing and is interchangeable with *estancia*. On the pampa, however, *hacienda* refers to livestock—cows, sheep, horses, and mules—although in earlier times it referred only to cattle. This originates in the fact that the wild cows and horses that once roamed the Argentine plains in their millions were considered state revenue—that is, the property of the royal *hacienda*, the Spanish treasury. Hence the building in Buenos Aires that houses the *Hacienda* is not the department of agriculture but the treasury building. *Ganado* is the word used for any stock of a single species; when an estancia has several types of livestock the term for it is not *los ganados* but *hacienda*.

Maté. It is to be lamented that in certain circles today—especially in those of Buenos Aires that ape European and North American ways—the drinking of maté is looked down on as something lower class and/or provincial. Nevertheless, maté continues to be the national beverage. In the past century, as drawings and paintings attest, it was drunk in the best society. Maté, in fact, is thoroughly and indelibly Argentine, a national institution, and not only is the literature of the last century permeated with it, but a rich and colorful treasury of popular sayings has grown up around it. (*Mate dulce*, "friendship"; *mate muy caliente*, "I too am burning with love"; *mate con miel*, "marriage.") More bewildering still is the fact that maté drinking is often condemned by the same people who admire everything else about the Argentine past, good and bad, with uncritical nationalistic fervor. The reality of maté lies in its chemistry. The infusion made of its leaves is rich in caffeine (as any Argentine studying for exams knows), tannin, protein, and citric and ascorbic acid, among other elements. For generations it enabled country dwellers to exist on a diet that amounted to little more than roasted meat. The Jesuits, who shepherded the Guarani Indians of Misiones Province and Paraguay, whence maté comes, were its great commercializers. One of them, Father Guevara, writing in the early eighteenth century, had this to say of its restorative properties: "Drinking *caá [yerba]* in these provinces is so common that neither cocoa, tea, nor coffee has ever become widespread. From the lowliest black slave to the noblest gentleman, everyone drinks maté. If a weary traveler turns up at the door of even a hovel or shack, maté will restore him; if he is sweating, maté will cool him; if he has thirst, maté will quench it; if he is sleepy, maté will wake him; if his head is burdened with cares, maté will lighten them; if his stomach is upset, maté will settle it."

Pampa. "All grass and sky, and sky and grass, and still more sky and grass," Cunninghame Graham wrote of the pampa. As a description it is perfect. The River Plate pampa, the grasslands of Uruguay and Argentina, are analogous to the prairies of North America, the steppes of the former Soviet Union, and the veld of South Africa. Often in English and seldom in Spanish, the word—for no good reason—is made plural. Writing in 1850, the poet Hilario Ascasubi noted that what the gaucho called the pampa was not the grassy plain of Buenos Aires Province but "the wilderness beyond the frontier garrisons, where nobody owns the land and the Indian tribes live and roam according to their state of savagery." La Pampa is also the name of an Argentine province, only part of which is pampa. *Los pampas* are the Indians of the pampa, a branch of the Araucanian family. The term is not ethnographically precise, for the history of Argentina's aboriginal population is an extremely complicated affair. A tribe's presence anywhere is no guarantee of its origin, since, as in North America, the Indians were driven from location to location by advancing whites. An *estaca pampa*, or Pampa Indian stake, is the ingenious way the Indians had of tying a horse on the treeless plain. The end of the rawhide tether was tied around a bone (or double-knotted if no bone could be found) and this was buried in a hole dug with a knife. The only way to loosen it was to pull it up vertically. The most haunting descriptions of the pampa are those in W. H. Hudson's masterpiece *Far Away and Long Ago*, which is still the best book written in English on Argentina.

Pulpería. A humble, rough-and-ready country store, saloon, and gathering place, with a thatched lean-to porch and a hitching post out front, the *pulpería*—according to Cunninghame Graham—was "the pampa club, news, calumny, and scandal take their rise in it, and there resort all the elite of frontier ruffianism." It was also where you could find "ponchos from Leeds, ready-made *calzoncillos*, *alpargatas*, figs, sardines, raisins, bread . . . saddle-cloths, and in a corner the *botillería*, where vermuth, absinthe, squarefaced gin, Carlón, and *vino seco* stand in a row, with the barrel of Brazilian caña, on the top of which the *pulpero* ostentatiously parades his pistol and his knife." Staples such as meat, sugar, tobacco, and maté were also on sale, and generations of gauchos and *paisanos* played cards and other games there. Some *pulperías* also doubled as staging posts, and on holidays various feats of horsemanship were performed in its vicinity. In the early days, a white flag run up a pole indicated that only drink and tobacco were available, while a red flag denoted that meat was also on hand. Drink was served from behind an iron or wooden grate. The most graphic portrayal of the nineteenth- and early-twentieth-century *pulpería*—like so many other aspects of Argentine country life—is perhaps to be found in the calender illustrations painted in the 1930s and 1940s by Florencio Molina Campos. Although they eschew realism, their documentary value is nonetheless unmatched.

Rodeo. The verb *rodear* in Spanish means "to surround"; so the *rodeo* is the action of surrounding, which, applied to livestock, is the roundup. In time, the place or piece of ground where cattle, horses, or sheep were brought together also became known as the *rodeo*. By extension, the animals rounded up and standing around are themselves referred to as the *rodeo*, so that in this sense the word has come additionally to mean the "herd." Cunninghame Graham records that the space of ground for the roundup was a quarter of a mile across, and that the animals were brought together almost every morning of the year. Writing of an earlier time, Félix de Azara, the Spanish naturalist, says the roundup was a weekly affair. Since the early estancias were started by taming wild cattle, to keep them from straying a herd was constantly rounded up and brought to a "home ground" that in time it grew accustomed to. Hence, a stamping ground.

Vaquería. The earliest horses—seventy-two in number, of a strain improved with Arab blood—had come from Andalusia to the Argentine with the first founding of Buenos Aires by Pedro de Mendoza, in 1536. Attacked, besieged, and starved out by Indians, the settlement was to fail within five years, and the remaining twelve horses, five of them mares, were set free. When Juan de Garay established a permanent settlement in 1580, it was estimated that these animals had multiplied to some eighty to one hundred thousand head. The cows had come with Garay from Paraguay. On the open rangeland, where there was neither wood nor stone to fence them in, they bred so prodigiously that they became literally countless. Azara estimated that at the beginning of the eighteenth century forty-eight million wild cattle roamed the pampa. In those times, since there was no way to preserve the meat, the animals were hunted and slaughtered in their thousands for grease and hides. Such hunts were known as *vaquerías*, and from 1609 on they were licensed. When carried out clandestinely, such operations were referred to as "cattle mining."

Norman Thomas di Giovanni